Britain's Butterflies

David Tomlinson

Rob Still

WILDGuides

First published 2002 by **WILD**Guides Ltd.

WILDGuides Ltd.
Parr House
63 Hatch Lane
Old Basing
Hampshire
RG24 7EB

www.wildguides.co.uk

ISBN 1-903657-03-2

Edited by Richard Fox & Martin Warren (Butterfly Conservation)
and Andy Swash (WildGuides)

Production and design by **WILD**Guides Ltd, Old Basing, Hampshire.
Printed in Hong Kong. The Hanway Press, London.

Contents

Foreword

Britain's butterflies are a rich part of our natural and cultural heritage, and most of us would admit to feeling uplifted at the sight of a butterfly dancing across a sunny meadow or delicately feeding from a garden flower. Many people's first memories of butterflies go hand in hand with recollections of warm summer days in a colourful, heavily scented garden complete with bumblebees and a trimmed lawn.

The butterflies attracted to nectar-rich garden flowers are only some of the 59 species that can be found in Britain and Ireland. This compact and beautifully illustrated guide has everything you need to identify the wild butterflies you may encounter in gardens, oakwoods, heathlands, downlands, and even the highest mountain moorlands. With its help you will be able to get the most from your butterfly observations from wingless juveniles through to spectacular adults.

This wonderful book is ideal for anyone who would simply like to be able to put a name to the butterflies they see, as well as being an excellent reference for the more dedicated naturalist or rambler. I hope it will inspire you to get out, as I do, and observe butterflies throughout the summer.

It's a sad fact that five of our native butterfly species are now extinct, and many, many others are in serious decline. But there is so much that each of us can do to help secure a future for butterflies, for example through butterfly-friendly gardening. Butterfly Conservation is the UK charity taking action to save our butterflies, moths and their habitats. Call 01929 400209 for more information about how you can get involved with their work and help conserve these fascinating creatures, or visit the website www.butterfly-conservation.org.

If you're anything like me, butterfly spotting will become an addictive and wonderfully fulfilling pastime. Without these bright insects, our world would be a duller place.

Alan Titchmarsh MBE, DL
Vice-president, Butterfly Conservation

Introduction

For sheer eye-catching beauty, it is difficult to think of a more perfect insect than a Red Admiral butterfly. The boldness of its design, the wonderful juxtaposition of black, red and white, the delicate blue wing-edging – a Red Admiral has it all. What is more, it is a superb flier, moving with grace and surprising power for a creature of such delicacy. It is also one of the commonest butterflies, and one you are likely to encounter almost anywhere in Britain.

Though there may be only a mere 60 or so species of butterflies that can be found regularly in Britain (fewer still in Ireland), spectacular species like the Red Admiral ensure continuing public interest in this group of insects. While many people find it difficult to get excited about beetles or spiders, butterflies are different. For many, an initial interest in butterflies is the catalyst for a wider enthusiasm for wildlife.

The aim of this book is simple: to not only make butterfly identification as straightforward as possible, but to get as many people as possible to take an interest in butterflies. Though there have been many books published on British butterflies, this is the first to use modern computer technology to show the caterpillar, chrysalis and adult stages of a butterfly's life-cycle on the same plate. The plates have been compiled using some of the very best in butterfly photography.

Few creatures are more sensitive indicators of the health of the environment than butterflies, and the continuing decline of so many species is a serious warning of the diminishing diversity of our countryside. Conserving butterflies is more than a case of simply protecting individual species, or providing isolated reserves. Instead, we have to consider the whole landscape, and how best we care for it and manage it.

Conservation depends upon popular support, as the more people who are interested in looking after our plants and animals the better for the health of the countryside and its wildlife. Therefore, we have been delighted to produce this book in association with Butterfly Conservation, the charity dedicated to saving butterflies, moths and their habitats in the UK and beyond. We hope that this book will inspire many more people to appreciate, understand and enjoy this beautiful and fascinating group of insects.

An introduction to butterflies and moths

Butterflies and moths are members of the huge family of some 165,000 insects known as the Lepidoptera. This is Greek and translates as 'wings with scales'. From it is derived the old-fashioned word *lepidopterist*, indicating someone who specialises in studying these insects.

Telling a butterfly from a moth is not always easy, for the two are closely related. Skipper butterflies, for example, are very moth-like in the way they perch. The easiest way to recognise a butterfly is to look at the antennae: those of butterflies have clubbed ends, whilst in moths they are fine and often feathery, without the clubbed end. In addition, a butterfly roosts with its wings closed tightly, held vertically above the body. In contrast, a moth usually roosts or rests with its wings folded horizontally flat over the body, the forewing largely obscuring the hindwing. Butterflies rarely fly at night, and many will only fly in bright sunshine. Moths fly mainly at night, but the few day-flying species can be readily recognised by their antennae and resting posture. The day-flying burnet moths have antennae that can be described as clubbed, but they always rest with their wings in the typical moth posture.

The day-flying Six spot Burnet moth with butterfly-like antennae

Butterflies reach their greatest diversity in the tropics. The islands of Trinidad and Tobago, for example, boast more than 600 species of butterflies, yet Britain and Ireland has only 60 species, despite the land-mass being 20 times greater. In Europe, there are some 440 species. New species are still being found world-wide as we study butterflies more carefully.

From top to bottom:
Puss Moth, note the 'feathered' antennae; Essex Emerald moth, note the thin antennae without clubbed ends, Dingy Skipper butterfly, quite moth-like in the way it rests, but note the 'clubbed' antennae; Adonis Blue butterfly, resting with wings closed typical of many butterflies but unlike most moths.

The butterfly body

Butterflies, like all other insects, have three distinct sections to their body: head, thorax and abdomen.

The **HEAD** is where a butterfly's sense organs are located: two *antennae*, two large compound *eyes* and a *proboscis*. The *antennae* are used for smell and balance; the *eyes* are able to discern colour and are especially good at sensing movement; the *proboscis* is a hollow, coiled tube through which the butterfly feeds. The *proboscis* can be uncoiled enabling a butterfly to reach deep into a flower for nectar.

The **THORAX** is the central and broadest of the three body sections and contains the muscles that operate the *wings* and *legs*. Most butterfly species have six *legs*, in three pairs, but some appear to have only two pairs, the first pair being very small and modified. The *wings* are made up of two extremely thin layers (upper and under) that are stretched across rigid veins through which blood flows. The wings are covered in microscopic scales that either reflect or refract light to give a range of colours and iridescence.

The **ABDOMEN** is where the digestive and reproductive organs are located. Generally speaking, the abdomen of a female butterfly is wider and broader than that of a male, to enable her to carry eggs. Females lay their eggs through the tip of the abdomen.

Pearl-bordered Fritillary (upperside)

Veins
Forewing
Abdomen
Thorax
Head

Hindwings

Antennae
Legs
Eye
Forewing
Hindwing
Proboscis
Veins

Clouded Yellow (underside)

9

The life-cycle of a butterfly

High Brown Fritillary

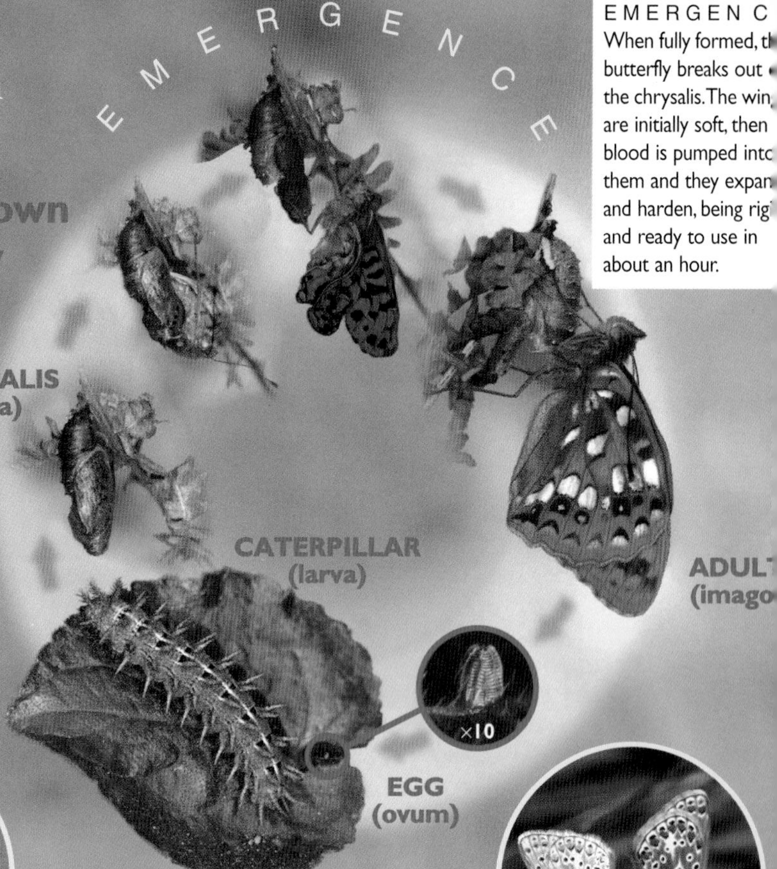

EMERGENCE
When fully formed, the butterfly breaks out of the chrysalis. The wings are initially soft, then blood is pumped into them and they expand and harden, being rigid and ready to use in about an hour.

CHRYSALIS (pupa)

A fully grown Brimstone caterpillar. Having moulted three times, and about to pupate, it has attached itself to the underside of a Buckthorn leaf and is spinning a silken girdle to support itself.

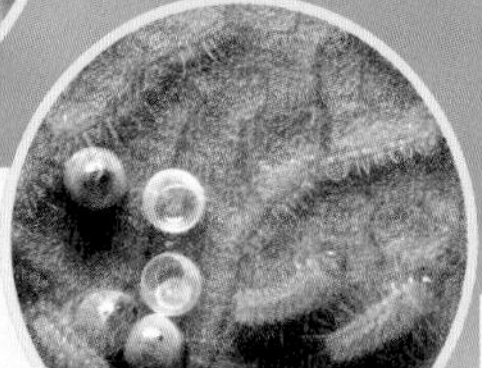

CATERPILLAR (larva)

ADULT (imago)

EGG (ovum)

×10

These freshly hatched Duke of Burgundy caterpillars will shed their skins four times before being fully-grown.

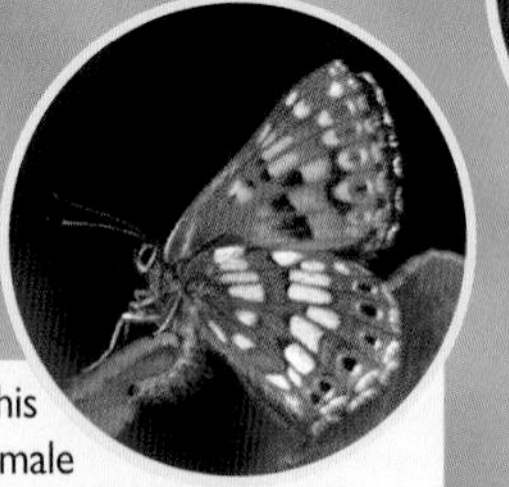

This female Duke of Burgundy will lay her eggs singly or in small groups of up to eight.

Upon emerging, male and female butterflies, like these Common Blues, will mate. After this, the female will spend as much time laying eggs as possible.

The life-cycle of all butterflies consists of four distinct stages: the **egg** (or ovum) hatches into the **caterpillar** (also known as the larva). The growing caterpillar moults several times, leaving its old skin behind. When fully-grown, it undertakes what is known as pupation, shedding its last skin and entering the third (and inactive) stage as a **chrysalis** (or pupa). A typical chrysalis is well camouflaged to avoid predators. Finally, the adult **butterfly** (or imago) emerges from the chrysalis.

EGG

Butterfly eggs come in many shapes and sizes depending on the species **(see pages 169-171)**.

Eggs are very small, usually less than 1 mm across their longest dimension. Although shapes, colours and sizes may differ, the structures are similar, comprising a hard outer case inside which is contained, much like a chicken's egg in miniature, an embryo surrounded by a nutritious fluid. Once fully formed, the caterpillar chews its way out of the egg, the remains of which are often eaten by the young caterpillar.

Eggs are laid singly, in small groups or large clusters, depending on the species involved. The eggs are almost always laid on, or very close to, the plant upon which the caterpillar will feed. The eggs usually hatch just over a week after being laid, except those that over-winter. About 95% of eggs laid hatch, the remainder being lost to adverse weather, victims of parasites or eaten by predators. Female butterflies take great care in selecting locations where their eggs are most likely to survive.

A cluster of Marsh Fritillary eggs.

CATERPILLAR

Once the caterpillar has emerged, it uses its strong jaws to feed on plant matter. Caterpillars come in many shapes, sizes and forms **(see pages 172-175)**. They are vulnerable and their look and behaviour is designed to maximise the chances of survival. Many are spiny or hairy to deter predators, some are poisonous, and some (such as the High Brown Fritillary that resembles a Bracken frond) are camouflaged to help them avoid being detected. In some species, caterpillars live together under the relative safety of a silken web, while other species live within blades of grass that they have rolled to create a tube. When small, caterpillars can fall victim to spiders and other insects, and, when larger, to birds and small mammals. Each species has a preferential plant or range of plants that it feeds on and many require very specific habitats and weather conditions. As they grow, caterpillars shed their flexible skin between three and six times, depending on the species. When fully-grown, the caterpillar anchors itself firmly and sheds its skin for the last time to reveal the young, soft chrysalis beneath.

Glanville Fritillary caterpillars venture to the top of their web to bask in sunshine.

At the latter stages of development all the parts of this Marbled White butterfly can be readily seen as the skin of the chrysalis becomes transparent.

CHRYSALIS

In time, the chrysalis hardens, whilst inside great changes are taking place: cells are re-arranging and new ones are being produced to create the adult butterfly. This transitional stage, otherwise known as pupation, is also fraught with danger. A large proportion of chrysali fall prey to birds and small mammals. Whilst some species form their chrysali on fence-posts and walls and are surprisingly conspicuous, the chrysali of others are well camouflaged. For example, the Black Hairstreak mimics a bird dropping (see page 14) and the White Admiral resembles a rolled-up Honeysuckle leaf. Others are formed in dense vegetation or leaf litter and some, like the skippers, spin silken cocoons around blades of grass in which they pupate **(see pages 176-178)**.

ADULT

After emergence, the adult takes up to an hour to expand its wings and be strong enough for flight. Once on the wing, the adult butterfly moves off to feed, find a mate and reproduce, starting the life-cycle all over again. Many butterflies have a remarkably short adult life. For a number of species, such as blues and hairstreaks, it can be as brief as four or five days. Others, such as the larger fritillaries and the Swallowtail, might live for two or even three weeks, but few survive as long as a Brimstone, which can live for up to ten months (although most of this time is spent in hibernation). Butterflies do not grow once they have emerged, and need to feed purely to maintain their strength to fly, find a mate and lay eggs.

Males often emerge before females. This head start gives them time to set up territories, and ensures that every emerging female is mated quickly. Once the female butterflies have laid their eggs, their biological function has been fulfilled. Male butterflies have a priority to mate with as many females as possible, and their patrolling flights are a constant search for virgin females. Males have special scales on the upperside of the forewings that produce scents (pheromones) which attract females. In most species, the wing patterns of males and females are significantly different to allow them to recognise one another.

The main threat to adult butterflies is predation. A wide range of bird species, including many summer visitors, time their breeding to coincide with peak insect emergence. Often you will see butterflies with parts of their wings missing, testimony to a narrow escape from, for example, a Spotted Flycatcher or Great Tit.

Both hindwings of this Small Tortoiseshell have a piece missing, probably as a result of a bird attempting to catch it whilst it rested with its wings closed.

Butterfly lifestyles

STRATEGIES FOR SURVIVAL

Timing of the life-cycle

The timing and duration of the life-cycle stages varies considerably from species to species. Many take a year to complete their life-cycle, others just a few weeks. Those that have shorter life-cycles may have two broods in a season, depending on the weather and other factors. In some species the adult butterflies hibernate, although the majority over-winter at the caterpillar or chrysalis stage. However, some skippers, blues and hairstreaks and the High Brown Fritillary spend the winter as eggs. In certain species, such as the Clouded Yellow, the interval between the egg being laid and the adult butterfly emerging from the chrysalis can be as little as four weeks.

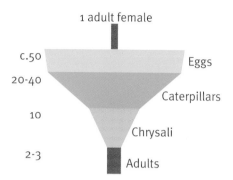

Butterfly survival

A female has the potential to lay several hundred eggs. However, many only live long enough to lay about 50 eggs, of which only 20-40 might hatch as caterpillars. Of these, perhaps 10 will survive to form chrysali, and of these 7-8 will perish, leaving just 1-3 adults (2–6%) surviving from the 50 eggs.

Over-wintering

Surviving the winter, in whatever stage, is a stern test. The entire population of most species exists in one stage only at this time. An exception is the Speckled Wood which over-winters as either chrysalis or caterpillar, the chrysalis hibernating and the caterpillars resting at the base of a plant, feeding if the temperature rises above 6°C.

Eggs that over-winter have thicker shells to withstand the cold. In some species, the over-wintering egg actually contains a fully formed caterpillar, hibernating in safety before emerging in the spring.

Some butterflies that over-winter in the caterpillar stage have adopted a strategy where the caterpillar spins a chamber of silken threads around vegetation, such as blades of grass or the leaves of the foodplant, in which they hibernate.

In species that over-winter as a chrysalis, these are often situated

Small Tortoiseshells hibernating in a garage.

close to the ground, in leaf litter or in thick vegetation, where the climatic conditions are more stable. Large and Small Whites over-winter as chrysali and can often be found on walls and under window ledges.

Over-wintering butterflies will feed avidly prior to hibernation, as they need to build up fat reserves to last them through the winter.

The Brimstone hibernates from August through to the first warm days of spring in February or March and chooses thick patches of Holly, Ivy and sometimes Bramble. The Small Tortoiseshell takes advantage of human dwellings and often uses unheated sheds, garages and lofts to pass the winter.

During the winter, adverse weather such as a prolonged freeze, damp spell or flooding can decimate a colony of butterflies.

Camouflage and defence

As well as the perils of adverse weather, butterflies fall victim to predators and parasites throughout their life-cycle.

In response, the caterpillars, chrysali and adults of some species have developed remarkable camouflage to help them avoid detection. As examples, caterpillars of the Purple Emperor resemble, in colour and markings, the leaves of the foodplant, and the Brimstone caterpillar lies along the midrib of a leaf and is not easy to find. As well as camouflage, some caterpillars have other defence mechanisms. Some are avoided by predators as they are poisonous, some are distasteful, and others are hairy or spiny and

The Black Hairstreak chrysalis, resembles a bird dropping and is therefore avoided by predators.

difficult to swallow. If approached, the very conspicuous Swallowtail caterpillar has a 'horn', which gives off an unpleasant smell, that it can extrude from its head.

In some species, such as the Green-veined White, the chrysalis forms to match the coloration of its surroundings, ranging from green to pale brown. Other species look like dead leaves, buds, seedpods and even bird droppings. All are a challenge to locate for even the most determined butterfly enthusiast.

The underside of an Orange-tip matches the dappled appearance of a favoured nectar plant.

Adult butterflies tend to be far more conspicuous than all the other life-cycle stages. They have to balance the demands of defending territories and looking for mates and egg-laying with the threat of predation. Females of many species are much less conspicuous than males. This reduces the risk of predation, thereby enabling more eggs to be laid. This strategy can be seen in wing coloration, such as the brown female blues, or behaviour, such as in female skippers and Marsh Fritillaries that rarely fly, preferring to stay hidden amongst the vegetation. Many species have 'eye' spots on their wings that deceive predators into thinking the butterfly is bigger than it actually is. The Peacock has the largest such 'eyes' of our butterflies and if a predator approaches the butterfly will open and close its wings rapidly to reveal these 'eyes', whilst making a scraping sound.

COLONIES

The majority of Britain's butterfly species live in discrete colonies. These are found in the same area year after year as long as suitable conditions exist. A butterfly, such as the Marsh Fritillary or Silver-spotted Skipper may appear common if there are large numbers in an area, but may be absent from other areas that appear suitable. Numbers also fluctuate between years, depending on breeding success and winter survival rates. These species' populations have a localised distribution. If a catastrophic event, such as a major change in land use, was to befall the colony it may become extinct and the site will not necessarily be recolonised. If these local extinctions become widespread, as in the cases of the Large Copper and the Large Blue, the species could be lost to Britain forever.

Individual colonies may have discernible differences from their near neighbours in terms of coloration and emergence times. Butterflies have a complex relationship with their surroundings and much still remains to be discovered. Recognising and understanding the fragile and complex nature of butterfly colonies and populations is essential to their future well-being.

A RELATIONSHIP WITH PLANTS
Foodplants

Female butterflies invariably lay their eggs on, or close to, their caterpillars' foodplant, which might be a flower, grass, shrub or tree. Most butterflies depend on just one or two favoured foodplants, though some are less fussy. Large Whites, for example, lay their eggs on a wide range of brassicas, including Cabbages, Kale and Brussels-sprouts, but they will also use garden Nasturtiums. Such flexibility has ensured the widespread success of this species, as well as its unpopularity with gardeners! In contrast, British Swallowtails

Different species have different needs

The conditions required to complete the life-cycle vary from species to species. One essential factor is a supply of the caterpillar foodplant growing in a suitable position.

Peacocks need large patches of Common Nettle and a rich supply of nectar plants, a combination that can be found anywhere in Britain and hence this is an abundant species.

Brimstones require Alder Buckthorn or Buckthorn (which are widespread in southern Britain), nectar plants and thickets of Ivy or Holly for hibernation. Its distribution closely matches that of its foodplant.

More complex, however, is the **Large Blue**, which needs rough grassland in which Wild Thyme grows and the ant *Myrmica sabuleti* occurs. Also, there must be an entrance to an ants' nest within 2 m of a Wild Thyme plant and furthermore, the grass must be less than 4 cm tall otherwise the habitat becomes unsuitable for the ant on which it depends.

lay their eggs almost exclusively on Milk-parsley, a very localised marshland plant, thus restricting where they can breed. Curiously, continental Swallowtails use a wide range of plants, chiefly of the Umbelliferae family, which explains why this butterfly is much more widespread abroad than it is in Britain. Similarly, six species of fritillary exclusively use violets and a further 12 British butterflies are reliant upon single caterpillar foodplant species. Those butterflies that rely on a single or limited range of foodplants that grow only in specific conditions are put at serious risk of local extinction by any changes in habitat that affect their foodplant.

Adult food sources

Most adult butterflies need nectar for survival, although some, including the Black Hairstreak and Purple Emperor, drink the sugary honeydew secretions left on leaves by aphids. The range of nectar plants used by some common butterflies is huge, whilst other butterflies use just a few species. The Small White uses a wide range, but is particularly attracted to both white and pink flowers. The Glanville Fritillary primarily uses Thrift but actively seeks out yellow flowers as well.

A RELATIONSHIP WITH ANTS

With a number of butterflies (particularly the blues) the life-cycle is linked intricately to that of certain species of ants.

The caterpillars of these species emit sweet liquids from a gland that attracts these ants day and night. The attendance of the ants helps the caterpillar's chances of survival, probably because the ants keep predators and parasites away.

Many of the blues have a strong relationship with ants, but none more so than the Large Blue, which is unable to survive without a particular species of red ant (*Myrmica sabuleti*) which takes the caterpillars into its nests. When the caterpillar is just a few millimetres long it drops from its foodplant to the ground and waits to be discovered by an ant. When discovered, the caterpillar releases a droplet of sweet liquid that the ant drinks before recruiting other worker ants into a feeding frenzy. After a period of up to four hours the caterpillar then adopts a posture which mimics an ant grub. This encourages the ant to pick up the caterpillar in its jaws and carry it into the ants' nest where it is deposited amongst the ant grubs. Such a practice does not benefit the ants in the long term, as the caterpillar spends the next few months feeding on ant grubs in the nest.

A red ant obtaining sweet secretions from a gland at the rear of a Chalkhill Blue caterpillar.

Movement and migration

MOVEMENT
Whilst most butterfly species live in colonies in specific habitats, 15 or so species range widely. These are the butterflies that are encountered most readily, such as the Small Tortoiseshell, Peacock, Brimstone and Large White. An average-sized garden, with the right plants will attract a dozen or more species. Always keep an eye out, as species will occasionally turn up in the most unlikely places.

MIGRATION
Though the majority of Britain's butterflies are resident, and many colonial species rarely move more than a few hundred metres from where they first emerged, a number are highly migratory. It is rare, for example, for Red Admirals to hibernate successfully in Britain, so the butterflies we see each summer are the offspring of migrants that have crossed the English Channel from the continent earlier in the season. Similarly, our populations of Clouded Yellows and Painted Ladies are dependent on migrants from the continent, as neither species is thought to over-winter successfully in Britain. Though the migration is principally northerly, there is a noticeable southward movement undertaken by such butterflies as Red Admirals and Painted Ladies in the autumn. Whether many (or any) manage to return to the continent is unknown.

Some butterflies only reach Britain as rare migrants. The best-known example is the Monarch, a migrant from North America, but several other species, such as the Long-tailed Blue and Camberwell Beauty, may wander to Britain, often wind-assisted, from the near continent.

RARITIES
Alhough this book covers all the butterflies that are likely to be found in Britain and Ireland, it does not include some of the extreme rarities that are occasionally recorded here as vagrants. Butterflies in this category include the Scarce Swallowtail, a stunning and widespread butterfly throughout southern Europe, and the Map, a common butterfly on the continent that can be found as close to Britain as Calais. Always be wary of more exotic species as they may have escaped from captivity.

Butterfly families

The butterflies that occur regularly in Britain can be divided into five families. Knowing these families is helpful in identification and this section provides a brief introduction.

Papilionidae

SWALLOWTAIL

SWALLOWTAIL (pages 36-37)
The Swallowtail is unmistakable due to its large size, bright black and yellow coloration and 'tails' on the hindwing.

Hesperiidae

LULWORTH SKIPPER

GRIZZLED SKIPPER

GOLDEN SKIPPERS (pages 32-41)
Golden skippers are unlike any other butterflies in Britain. Small and moth-like, with large eyes, short wings and a broad body, they have very flexible forewings that enable them to fly with great agility and speed, flitting between flowers – hence their name.
They often rest in a characteristic pose with hindwings flat and forewings raised.

SKIPPERS (pages 30-31, 42-45)
Skippers differ from golden skippers as they hold their wings flat. Otherwise they are similar in size, body shape and behaviour. All skipper caterpillars feed in a protective tent of vegetation held together with silken threads.

Pieridae

WOOD WHITE   CLOUDED YELLOW   BRIMSTONE   LARGE WHITE

WOOD WHITES (pages 48-51)
Delicate and with a fluttering flight, wood whites are medium-sized butterflies with long, slim bodies and long, oval wings.

CLOUDED YELLOWS (pages 52-53, 162-163)
A migratory group of fast-flying, very similar species. The three species that reach Britain have very distinctive caterpillars.

BRIMSTONE (pages 54-55)
Large size, yellow coloration and with a distinctive wing shape, this is the only British member of the Pieridae family to hibernate as an adult.

WHITES (pages 56-63)
Medium- to large-sized butterflies with mainly white wings. The whites are the only members of this group to bask with their wings open

Lycaenidae

SMALL COPPER · SILVER-STUDDED BLUE · DUKE OF BURGUNDY

WHITE-LETTER HAIRSTREAK

HAIRSTREAKS
(pages 64-73)
Small and elusive, all
except the Green
Hairstreak have 'tails'
and a distinctive
white 'hairstreak' line
on their underside.

COPPERS
(pages 74-75)
Small, highly
conspicuous, fast-
flying butterflies with
distinctive shining
copper-orange and
brown wings.

BLUES
(pages 76-93)
Small butterflies with
blue upperwings,
although females
(and males of some
species) are brown.
All have spotted
underwings.

DUKE OF BURGUNDY
(pages 94-95)
Resembles a fritillary,
but its small size and
fast, whirring flight
distinguish it. The
males only use four
legs, the females all
six.

Nymphalidae

COMMA

PEARL-BORDERED FRITILLARY

RINGLET

EMPERORS, ADMIRALS AND ALLIES (pages 96-109)
This group of large, strong-flying butterflies has underwings that are designed for camouflage contrasting with colourful upperwings. They have four functioning legs.

FRITILLARIES (pages 110-125)
A group of medium- to large-sized butterflies with a flitting flight and distinctive black-on-orange patterned upperwings. Their underwings have intricate patterns of white, silver, orange and brown.

BROWNS (pages 126-147)
A diverse group of small- to large-sized butterflies, the browns all have black 'eye' spots on the upperside and underside of the forewing. They are generally brown and orange coloured except for the Marbled White.

Lepidopterists place each individual species of butterfly within a group, or family, of similar species, depending on its taxonomy.

The relationship is usually quite apparent. The Common Blue and the Adonis Blue, for example, are clearly closely related, and are members of the Lycaenidae. This group also includes the hairstreaks, which appear different but share many similarities with the blues.

It is usually relatively easy to place a butterfly within its family, and this is one of the first steps to correct identification. However, there are number of species that can catch out the unwary.

The Nymphalidae, for example, includes many different species, and these are split into groups of butterflies with similar characteristics. The Marbled White is in fact a brown: although it may not look as if it belongs in this family, its structure, life-cycle and habits clearly place it here.

19

Butterfly habitats

Butterflies have evolved to occupy almost every wild and semi-natural habitat in Britain: they are usually very rare in extensive areas of intensive arable farming, plantations of exotic trees, and inhospitable places like exposed mountains. The key to finding many species of butterflies is knowing which habitat or habitats they prefer.

GARDENS AND PARKS

A favoured habitat for many species, with a third of Britain's butterflies being recorded regularly in gardens. Though the majority of butterflies use these habitats only for feeding, some will also breed in gardens if suitable foodplants are available. Species that occur most frequently include the whites, Holly Blue, Small Tortoiseshell, Red Admiral and Comma, while in rural gardens, Orange-tips and Meadow Browns often pass through.

HEDGEROWS AND FARMLAND

Mixed farmland can be a productive place to find a wide variety of butterflies. The hedgerows and banks provide a favoured habitat for Orange-tips, Ringlets, Gatekeepers, skippers and Small Coppers, while hay meadows may hold Meadow Browns, Common Blues and perhaps Clouded Yellows. The latter is generally the only butterfly to be found in extensive fields of Lucerne or clover.

Many butterflies like ground that is lightly grazed by livestock, and so a number of butterfly reserves are managed by grazing. Intensive arable farms have little attraction for butterflies, unless they contain hedgerows and flowery margins.

Roadside verges and areas of rough grassland or meadows can be good for butterflies. The best hedgerows are those that are not flailed every year, have a variety of different shrubs and are adjacent to flower-rich meadows. This combination of foodplants and nectar sources is attractive to many species.

DOWNLAND

Some of our rarest and most attractive butterflies, such as the Chalkhill Blue, Adonis Blue and Silver-spotted Skipper, are to be found on the downs of southern England. This is usually because their foodplants flourish best on chalk, while the south-facing slopes of downs have their own warm micro-climate, making them attractive to sun-loving species that are on the northern edge of their European range.

Downland butterflies are at their most conspicuous on warm, windless days when different species will patrol their territories, perch on exposed branches or bask in the sunshine. If it is windy, most species stay on the ground amongst vegetation. Butterflies, often of more than one species, roost in groups in the early evening; they bask in the early morning sun for a few minutes before flying off.

Many areas of downland were lost in the latter part of the 20th century when they were ploughed and cereal crops grown. Whilst ploughing invariably destroys the habitat, it can also be lost when traditional grazing by sheep or cattle ceases. Scrub then develops, shading out the favoured foodplants. Certain species prefer different intensities of grazing from others, so management practices have to take this into account.

MANAGED WOODLAND

A wide variety of butterflies flourish in coppiced or managed woodland, but they soon disappear where the canopy is allowed to cover over and exclude the light. It was the decline in coppicing that is thought to have led to the extinction of the High Brown Fritillary in eastern England. The Heath Fritillary still flourishes at Blean Woods in Kent only because regular coppicing takes place. Several other species depend on woodlands where coppicing or ride-clearing is practised. The Wood White, for example, has survived in several southern woodlands where rides are regularly cut amongst forestry plantations.

MATURE WOODLAND

Several British butterflies, such as the Silver-washed Fritillary, White Admiral, Wood White and Purple Emperor, are restricted to woodland, but all also need rides and open areas if their populations

The best woodlands for butterflies are those that have a mosaic of habitats, including forest clearings, rides and mature trees. Bramble is an extremely popular nectar source for woodland species. Remember that there are a number of canopy-dwelling butterflies, which do not descend regularly, and so binoculars are essential. Rides and glades are good for observing patrolling males, and spending time near foodplants, for example violets, is a good way of seeing fritillaries and other species well.

are to survive. Several of the hairstreaks are also typically woodland inhabitants, though butterflies such as the Purple Hairstreak may spend their entire adult life centred on a single mature oak.

HEATHLAND AND MOORLAND
Like downland, heathland depends upon management for its survival. Many heaths of southern England have been destroyed or fragmented during the past century. Even so, heathland provides a vital habitat for a number of species, including the Grayling, Small Heath and Silver-studded Blue. The latter can sometimes be found in huge numbers on certain southern heathlands.

Exmoor and Dartmoor provide an important refuge for many butterflies, including almost all the fritillaries. The endangered High Brown Fritillary occurs on both moors, while Exmoor's populations of Heath Fritillaries were only discovered recently. Northern moorlands are generally much less productive for butterflies but can be good for Dark Green and Small Pearl-bordered Fritillaries.

WETLAND AND FENLAND
These are habitats with few specialist British butterflies. One exception is the Swallowtail, which is confined to the Norfolk Broads where its food plant, Milk-parsley, grows in abundance. Our other marshland species, the Large Copper, is now extinct in Britain.

UPLANDS
The hills and mountains of northern Britain typically have too harsh a climate for butterflies to survive. However, there are a few hardy species that can be found in the uplands, of which the classic examples are the Mountain Ringlet and Large Heath.

COASTAL DUNES AND CLIFFS
Because these are habitats largely unchanged by man's activities, several species thrive in them. Glanville Fritillaries are restricted almost entirely to the cliffs of the Isle of Wight, while several species, such as Common Blue, Dark Green Fritillary, Wall and Grayling, thrive in coastal dunes.

While heathland and moorland butterflies are generally colonial, the Grayling, a heath and dune specialist can be encountered in any dry area where there is exposed sand or soil. Finding the foodplant and searching on calm, sunny days will increase your chances of seeing species such as Large Heath and Mountain Ringlet.

Gardening for butterflies

More than 20 different species of butterfly, a third of those that occur in Britain, are found regularly in gardens. These range from the Red Admiral and Orange-tip that generally just wander through rural gardens, to species like the Holly Blue and Small Tortoiseshell that often breed.

It is possible to attract a variety of butterflies to even the smallest urban garden by providing a few attractive nectar plants. However, careful planting of large gardens with both nectar-providing plants and suitable flowers, grasses and trees upon which butterflies can lay their eggs will attract a considerable variety of species, and help conservation. A list of butterflies, their favoured caterpillar foodplants and adult food sources can be found on pages 179-181.

When planning a butterfly garden, remember that these insects require sun, warmth and shelter. Whilst no butterfly garden is complete without buddleias, many other species will also attract butterflies, including Aubretia, Sweet-William, violets, French Marigolds, Lobelia, Honesty, Lavender, marjoram and Valerian. In wild areas, Bramble, thistles, Bugle, dandelions, Blackthorn, willows, Wild Privet, Ivy and Common Nettles can all be important. There are some excellent books published on the subject if you would like further advice (see page 183).

As well as nectar plants for adults, don't forget the caterpillars; an area of coarse grasses including Cock's-foot for browns; patches of Common Bird's-foot-trefoil in short grass, if your garden soil is suitable, for Common Blue and stands of Common Nettle for Small Tortoiseshell and Peacock.

Butterfly watching and photography

Butterfly collecting – an enthusiasm of many people in Victorian times – has largely given way to butterfly watching today. Like birdwatchers, the butterfly watcher can get as much out of the hobby as he or she wishes. Many people simply like looking at butterflies, others enjoy recording butterflies in their garden, parish or county, while more serious enthusiasts make visits to specific areas in the hope of seeing rare species. It is possible to see all of Britain's breeding butterflies in a single season, but to do so takes careful planning, a lot of travelling, and a certain amount of luck with the weather.

We can only learn about how butterfly populations are changing if accurate records are kept. Keen butterfly watchers are urged to send their records to local branches of Butterfly Conservation or county recorders (see pages 26-27 and 183).

Butterfly sites

As well as looking locally, visiting sites that are known to have many butterflies at the right time of year and in the right weather conditions can be very rewarding. These areas are often within nature reserves. There are also a number of well-known sites that butterfly watchers visit in order to find certain rare or localised species, and several of these are given in this book. For details of where to look for certain species, check with your county Wildlife Trust, or obtain information from books or the Internet.

Techniques and tips

A surprising number of butterflies are tame and approachable, allowing close

and sometimes prolonged observation. Others are much more difficult to watch: male Dark Green Fritillaries, for example, are so active that they rarely seem to land. Learn about the behaviour of the butterfly you are seeking before looking for it, as this will allow you to plan your approach. It is worth noting whether the butterfly you are looking for will fly in overcast conditions, or requires strong sunshine. For example, there is little point in looking for Mountain Ringlets unless the sun is bright, yet sunshine is often rare in July in the mountains and fells where this butterfly lives. Several species are best looked for in the early hours of the morning, when they are most active.

Equipment

The most useful item of equipment is a close-focussing binocular. An increasing number of quality binoculars will focus down to within a metre or so, and these are ideal for butterfly watching. Magnification hardly matters as long as the binocular focuses close enough, but 7× or 8× is ideal. A telescope mounted on a tripod can be useful for observing hairstreaks that spend most of their lives high in the canopy.

Although most British butterflies can be readily identified without being caught, serious lepidopterists often carry a butterfly net, allowing individual butterflies to be captured, identified and studied at close quarters. A glass-bottomed pillbox complements the net. Though you can make your own net, it is much easier to buy one ready-made from a supplier of entomological equipment. Nets come in a variety of shapes and sizes. A folding net is handy, as it can be stowed in a rucksack, or even a coat pocket, when not needed.

Photography

Traditional methods of photography are changing fast with the introduction of digital cameras. However, all the photographs illustrating this book were taken with 35 mm single-lens reflex cameras, using transparency film. This is still the best way to capture images of butterflies that are suitable for reproduction in books or magazines. It is possible to take highly satisfactory photographs using a standard 50 mm lens and natural light, but short telephoto lenses (105 mm to 200 mm), preferably with a macro facility, are most popular with serious butterfly photographers.

Many photographers breed butterflies in captivity and photograph the freshly emerged adults soon after hatching when they are still perfect. Care should be taken to return such bred butterflies back to their home site. Flash is often used in butterfly photography, as this not only provides an instant source of light, but also gives an increased depth of field, an important requirement in close-up or macro photography. Flash photography is a specialised art and requires both practice and experimentation: professionals will often use two flash heads to give the natural-looking lighting that they require.

Butterfly Conservation

Founded in 1968, Butterfly Conservation is the UK charity taking action to save butterflies, moths and their habitats.

Britain has 59 regularly seen butterfly species with several more that visit us regularly from abroad to breed. Over the last fifty years, many species of butterfly and moth have declined dramatically in both abundance and range. More than half our native butterfly species are now under threat and five are already extinct in the UK. There have been many local extinctions and few butterflies are as common as they once were. Several are very restricted in their range: for example, the Swallowtail to parts of the Norfolk Broads, the Glanville Fritillary to the Isle of Wight and the Adonis Blue to parts of our southern chalk downs. Rapid and alarming declines have often arisen because of changes in agriculture and forestry practices.

Even our common butterflies have become severely reduced in number, and, for many people, butterflies are no longer an intrinsic part of summer days. Their loss is symptomatic of the exploitation of the environment that has occurred and is continuing.

Butterfly Conservation runs a wide variety of conservation projects, and is taking the lead in conserving the UK's butterfly and moth populations, particularly through the preparation of Species Action Plans and Regional Action Plans. These plans are implemented in close collaboration with statutory and voluntary conservation organisations, as well as with corporate partners and individuals.

In addition, Butterfly Conservation has developed a strategy to protect important butterfly and moth populations through the establishment of reserves. These may be wholly or jointly owned, but may also be land belonging to individuals and organisations where we advise on habitat maintenance, or land which is managed by our local branches and other volunteers.

A strong membership makes up 32 branches throughout the UK. Every year, these branches organise field trips, talks, and educational courses across the country. Volunteers are involved in monitoring hundreds of important localities, and give practical help by attending work-parties to manage habitats.

An informative and colour illustrated magazine for members is published three times a year and acts as a forum for the exchange of information and views. Occasional papers are published which offer more detailed scientific news and research. Local branches also produce their own regular newsletters providing general information and articles of local interest.

Additional information can be found on Butterfly Conservation's website.

JOIN BUTTERFLY CONSERVATION AND HELP STOP THE DECLINE

You can directly support us in this vital work by joining Butterfly Conservation. With an annual membership you will receive our award-winning magazine *Butterfly Conservation News* three times a year and membership of your local branch of Butterfly Conservation.

For a membership application form, or for further information, please contact us at:
Butterfly Conservation, Manor Yard, East Lulworth, Wareham, Dorset BH20 5QP
Tel: 01929 400 209   Fax: 01929 400 210
Website: www.butterfly-conservation.org   Email: info@butterfly-conservation.org

BUTTERFLY RECORDING AND MONITORING

Butterflies can only be conserved if we know where they are and why they are threatened. Butterfly Conservation organises a range of recording and monitoring projects, relying almost entirely on volunteer recorders to provide this vital information. The observations of volunteer recorders contribute directly to the efforts to save these beautiful creatures. Butterfly Conservation would welcome your help!

Each recording and monitoring project uses a different method to meet the different conservation challenges facing particular butterflies. They also vary in the amount of time and level of expertise needed to take part. There are two main projects – *Butterflies for the New Millennium* for sightings of butterflies made anywhere (from urban gardens to mountain summits) and *Butterfly Transects* along specific routes.

Butterflies for the New Millennium

With the Butterflies for the New Millennium project, you can record butterflies whenever and wherever you see them, whether in your garden, on walks through the countryside or on holiday in a different part of Britain. This project was launched in 1995 to carry out a detailed survey of the distribution of all butterfly species across Britain and Ireland and so to provide up-to-date information for conservation and research. Over 10,000 volunteers have taken part so far and their sightings have been used to produce The Millennium Atlas of Butterflies in Britain and Ireland (published by Oxford University Press in 2001).

Anyone can help, you don't have to be an expert and a free Butterflies for the New Millennium information pack is available from Butterfly Conservation. All butterfly species are covered by the project and you can record anywhere in Britain and Ireland. Standard forms are used to note down the identity and number of any butterflies that you see, the date, and the name and grid reference of the place where they were seen. Records are returned to volunteer county co-ordinators (listed in the information pack and on the Butterfly Conservation website). Many areas remain under-recorded and there are undoubtedly many colonies of rare species still to be discovered – it is not too late to become involved!

Butterfly Transects

Butterfly transects are the most scientific and accurate way to check how butterfly populations are faring on individual sites. A transect is a walk around a particular area (perhaps a favourite walk near your home) during which counts are made of the butterflies seen. The route remains the same each time and the transect is walked during fine weather every week from April until the end of September. This requires a considerable time commitment from volunteer recorders, although transects can be shared by groups of people each walking a certain number of weeks. Recorders also need to be reasonably confident of their ability to identify butterflies.

The information gained from transect monitoring is immensely useful, especially if the same transect is walked for many years. It not only provides a detailed assessment of how each species is doing every year, but a huge amount has been discovered about the ecology of butterflies and how habitat management and the weather affect their populations. Further information can be found on Butterfly Conservation's website.

Saving butterflies, moths and their habitats.

BUTTERFLY CONSERVATION

27

How to identify butterflies

Most species of butterfly found in Britain are relatively straightforward to identify. Some are less so and require close observation. However, with experience, even these species are readily identified. There are a few species that are a challenge to even the most knowledgeable butterfly watcher but generally these are rare butterflies. There is also the enigma of the Real's Wood White, only identified as occurring in Ireland in 2001 but not found in Britain as yet...

The key to identifying butterflies is knowing the combination of features that need to be seen, and an understanding of habitat preferences, flight periods and behaviour.

Which Family?
Working out which family the butterfly belongs to is a good start (see pages 18-19). For example, if a fritillary is encountered it is readily recognisable by its distinctive black-and-orange upperwings. The next step is to observe the underwing to confirm the species' identification.

Habitat and location
A knowledge of which habitats are favoured by which butterflies is helpful. A hairstreak seen on elm, for example, is extremely unlikely to be a Black Hairstreak, and will almost certainly be a White-letter Hairstreak.

Flight period
Some similar butterflies fly at different times and this can help identification. A golden skipper seen in early June is more likely to be a Large Skipper than a Small Skipper, and almost certainly not an Essex Skipper, which does not usually fly until the very end of June.

Behaviour and jizz
Some butterflies have a indefinable 'look' peculiar to that particular species known as jizz. For example, the wing shape of a flying Brimstone is an obvious identifier, even if only seen fleetingly. Dark Green and High Brown Fritillaries have subtle differences in the jizz of their flight which can be learned with experience.

Experience
A combination of factors, learned over time will help to ensure a speedy identification. For example, having identified a brown butterfly seen in late May as being of the blue family, a combination of location, flight period, knowledge of coloration and jizz will help confirm identification.

Be Wary!
Butterflies can turn up in unexpected places. Species that are increasing in numbers will colonise areas from which they were previously absent. Some rare migrants, at first glance, resemble common butterflies. Never rely on one factor alone to confirm the identification of a difficult species.

Finding eggs, caterpillars and chrysali
Essential to the finding of early life stages is an understanding of where different species lay their eggs, an ability to identify the foodplants the caterpillars require and a knowledge of pupation sites.

The following plates and text cover all the information you need to identify Britain's butterflies at all stages of their life-cycle.

How to use this guide

All the butterflies that are recorded regularly in the British Isles are depicted in the following plates. The accompanying text follows a consistent format, as outlined below:

English name
Scientific name

IDENTIFICATION:
ADULT : A concise description of the adult butterfly, detailing the key identification features to look for.

CHRYSALIS , CATERPILLAR and EGG : Brief descriptions of the three early stages of the butterfly's life-cycle.

BEHAVIOUR:
Summarises the key aspects of the behaviour of the species, which can often be a clue to identification.

HABITAT:
Many butterflies are restricted to certain habitats, as indicated here.

POPULATION AND CONSERVATION:
A résumé of the butterfly's current status in the Britain and Ireland.

THE PLATES
Pictured at 1·5× life size are the adult butterfly, showing typically both upperside and underside, and both sexes when they differ significantly. In addition, the caterpillar and chrysalis are shown, along with the foodplant. Note that certain species, such as Grayling and Clouded Yellow, almost never settle with their wings open.
Annotations on the plate identify the following:

STATUS

	Threatened Resident

MEASUREMENTS
Each species' vital statistics in millimetres. Eggs are width (w) × height (h).

Wingspan:	male 29 mm
	female 31 mm
Chrysalis:	16 mm
Caterpillar:	25 mm
Egg:	0·6 (w) × 0·5 mm (h)

LIFE-CYCLE CHART
Pie-chart, showing the months when the various stages in the butterfly's life-cycle occur. **Yellow** represents the egg, **green** the caterpillar, **orange** the chrysalis and **red** the adult. Shaded colour indicates lower abundance, full colour indicates peak abundance.
The flight period of the adult is duplicated in the centre circle to allow a full view of the life-cycle.

DISTRIBUTION MAP
Map showing the current distribution of the species within Britain and Ireland.

WHERE TO FIND
Information on the best locations and specific sites to find the species.

OBSERVATION TIPS
Clues as to how to go about finding and watching the species to help you get the best from your butterfly watching.

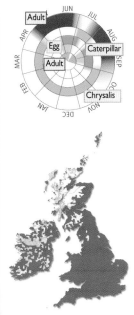

WHERE TO FIND
Check suitable habitat with oak trees anywhere within range: this is one of the most overlooked of our butterflies.

OBSERVATION TIPS
Best looked for in late May, when numbers peak; fine weather is best for success.

M male		**F** female		**Ad** adult	
Ch chrysalis		**Ca** caterpillar			

Other annotations specific to the plate are explained in the accompanying text.

Chequered Skipper
Carterocephalus palaemon

Though extinct in England since 1976, colonies of this attractive species can still be found in western Scotland.

Threatened Resident

Wingspan:	male 29 m
	female 31 m
Chrysalis:	16 m
Caterpillar:	25 m
Egg:	0·6 (w) × 0·5 mm (

IDENTIFICATION

ADULT : With its distinctive chequered cream-on-chocolate wings, this is one of the easiest of the skippers to identify. The only possible confusion is with the Duke of Burgundy (*page 94*), but the latter has a distinctively different shape and is spotted rather than chequered, and its British range is nowhere near that of the Chequered Skipper.

CHRYSALIS : Hidden amongst dead leaves, and resembles a dead blade of grass, so extremely difficult to find.

CATERPILLAR : Dark green with pale lines before hibernation; after hibernation, pale sepia with pinkish-white lines.

EGG : Off-white, laid singly on grass blades. In Scotland the main foodplant is Purple Moor-grass.

BEHAVIOUR

The male establishes a small territory, darting from his favoured perch in a blur of wings to investigate intruders. Like all skippers, the flight is fast and dashing, with sudden changes of direction. Both sexes visit flowers, and seem particularly keen on blue species, including Bugle and Bluebell and Marsh Thistle.

HABITAT

Scottish colonies are generally in open grassland on the edge of broad-leaved woodland. Wet but not waterlogged soils are preferred, and most breeding areas are found close to the base of a slope, and usually close to a loch or river. In England, the Chequered Skipper used to favour woodland rides and clearings.

POPULATION AND CONSERVATION

Once a scarce but widespread species in the English Midlands, the last known colony died out in 1976 and subsequent reintroductions have, so far, been unsuccessful. The Scottish colonies, first discovered in 1942, are holding their own in ten core areas.

WHERE TO FIN
Argyll, where there ar
some 40 known colonie
Glasdrum Wood, Loc
Creran, Strathclyde is
reliable site

OBSERVATION TIP
Best looked for in lat
May, when numbers pea
fine weather is best fc
success. In wet weather
is still worth checkir
flower-heads for restir
adult

Small Skipper

Thymelicus sylvestris

A common and widespread colonial butterfly of rough grassland and woodland glades.

Common Resident

Wingspan:	27–34 mr
Chrysalis:	16–20 mr
Caterpillar:	20–25 m
Egg:	0·85 (w) x 0·5 mm (F

IDENTIFICATION

ADULT : Despite its name, this is not our smallest skipper. It is best identified by its unmarked golden-orange wings, though the forewing of the male carries a distinctive dark line (sex brand). The wings lack the faint mottling of the Large Skipper, but check the colour of the tips of the antennae (dull brown or orange) to separate from the very similar Essex Skipper *(page 34)*.

CHRYSALIS : Green, and formed near the ground.

CATERPILLAR : Green, with a dark green line along the back. The head is large and green.

EGG : Initially white, yellowing with age, and laid in small clusters on the foodplant, Yorkshire-fog. The egg hatches in August, unlike that of the Essex Skipper which does not hatch until the following spring.

BEHAVIOUR

A colonial species. The male Small Skipper is a highly skilled flier, travelling at great speed in a blur of golden wings, and frequently demonstrating great manoeuvrability. Much more secretive than the Large Skipper. Females are both sedentary and unobtrusive.

HABITAT

This is an adaptable butterfly, occurring wherever tall clumps of Yorkshire-fog grow. It prefers more open sites than the Large Skipper, often being found in rough grassland on roadside verges, at the edges of fields or in woodland glades.

POPULATION AND CONSERVATION

Common and widespread, with considerable extension of range northwards in recent decades.

WHERE TO FINE
Look for Yorkshire-fog an you should find th butterfl

OBSERVATION TIP:
Remember that this is secretive species, and even in a large colony only small number c individuals may be visibl at one time

Essex Skipper

Thymelicus lineola

This skipper is widespread in south-east England where it is increasing its range.

Common Resident

Wingspan:	26–30 m
Chrysalis:	15–17 m
Caterpillar:	20–24 m
Egg:	0·8 (w) x 0·3 mm

IDENTIFICATION

Adult : Virtually identical in appearance to the Small Skipper, except that the Essex Skipper Esx has distinctive glossy black tips to its antennae, whereas those of the Small Skipper Sml are dull brown or orange. With practice it is also possible to separate the two by the more pointed wings of the Essex Skipper. In addition, the male's sex brand on the forewing tends to be shorter, straighter and finer than that of the Small Skipper.

Chrysalis : Pale green, and formed at the base of the foodplant.

Caterpillar : Green with white stripes, but the striped head separates it from the Small Skipper.

Egg : Pearly white when laid. The egg does not hatch until the following spring, when the emerging caterpillar feeds on Cock's-foot or other grasses.

BEHAVIOUR

A colonial species, and very similar in behaviour to the Small Skipper. Like the latter, the male is much more active than the female, flying rapidly and demonstrating remarkable manoeuvrability in the air. Its flight tends to be ground-hugging, except when courting a female. Like other skippers, the Essex likes to roost communally, and often several butterflies will gather on the same grass stem.

HABITAT

Tall, dry grassland growing in open but sunny situations suits this skipper best. It is fond of roadside verges, woodland rides, sea walls and embankments.

POPULATION AND CONSERVATION

Because of its similarity to the Small Skipper the Essex Skipper has been much overlooked in the past, but this butterfly is faring well and has expanded its range considerably in recent years.

WHERE TO FIN
Though first describe
from Essex (where
remains widespread),
can be found common
from Dorset
Lincolnshir

OBSERVATION TIP
The black tips to th
antennae are suprising
easy to see in the fiel
Peak numbers occur
late July, a week later th
the Small Skipp

Lulworth Skipper

Thymelicus acteon

As its name suggests, this skipper is a speciality of south-east Dorset, but it is far more widespread on the continent

Localised Resident

Wingspan: male 24–27 mr
female 25–28 mr
Chrysalis: 17 mr
Caterpillar: 25 mr
Egg: 0·8 (w) x 1.6 mm (f

IDENTIFICATION

ADULT : The smallest and darkest of the 'golden' skippers (the group that includes Large, Small and Essex). Look for the so-called 'sun-ray' on the forewing of the female – a bright circle of golden marks on a dark background. The dark, almost olive-coloured wings distinguish the male.

CHRYSALIS : Pale green and hidden in a tussock of grass.

CATERPILLAR : Green, with a dark line along the middle of the back and a pale yellowish line on either side. Usually hidden in a feeding tube.

EGG : The pale, oblong egg is laid in rows on the flower sheath of its only foodplant, Tor-grass.

BEHAVIOUR

Lives in self-contained colonies, with little or no interchange between them. Some colonies can be huge, containing hundreds of thousands of individuals. Flies only in strong sunshine, when becomes extremely active, feeding with enthusiasm on any plants in flower, especially Wild Marjoram, Bramble and ragworts.

HABITAT

Unimproved and unfertilised grasslands on chalk downland, coastal grassland and undercliffs. Areas of tall grass are essential.

POPULATION AND CONSERVATION

This butterfly has always been restricted in Britain to south Dorset and a few sites in Devon. Its population is stable overall and although there have declines in some areas, many large colonies flourish.

WHERE TO FIND

South Dorset coas
Usually found on south
facing slopes shelterer
from onshore winds. On
of the biggest colonies i
located around Lulwort
Cove, while others are
close to the coas
between Swanage an
Weymouth

OBSERVATION TIP

Look for this species on
hot summer days. It is a
its most abundant in earl
to mid-Augus

Silver-spotted Skipper

Hesperia comma

A rare and localised skipper, characteristic of the chalk downlands of southern England, the northern edge of its European range.

Localised Resident

Wingspan: male 29–34 mr
female 32–37 mr
Chrysalis: 15 mm
Caterpillar: 25 mm
Egg: 0·9 (w) x 0·7 mm (h

IDENTIFICATION

ADULT : Both sexes are readily identified by the dozen or so silver spots on the underside of each hindwing, easily seen when the butterfly is at rest. These are the best way to separate it from the Large Skipper (*page 40*), with which it has long been confused. However, the flight periods of the two species hardly overlap; the Silver-spotted is the last of the skippers to emerge, usually not appearing until the second week of August, by which time most Large Skippers have disappeared.

CHRYSALIS : Dark, protected by a cocoon in a grass tussock.

CATERPILLAR : Dark sepia-green and distinctly unattractive, spinning its own silk nest.

EGG : The pale egg is laid exclusively on Sheep's-fescue, the sole foodplant.

BEHAVIOUR

A sun-worshipping species that spends much of its short adult life basking on bare ground. It holds its wings in the characteristic way of all 'golden' skippers. The flight is fast and darting, the butterflies feeding on late summer flowers such as Dwarf Thistle and knapweeds.

HABITAT

Open chalk grassland, ideally heavily grazed by sheep or rabbits to produce a short, sparse turf. Usually found on south-facing slopes, but if it can find warm enough conditions it will also occur on other scarps.

POPULATION AND CONSERVATION

This butterfly has always been restricted to chalk and limestone grassland but has declined drastically since the 1950s. Habitat conservation requires grazing by stock to reduce the reliance on rabbits. It does not survive well on small, isolated sites. The current population trend is upward due to conservation efforts and, possibly, climate change.

WHERE TO FIND

Eight main centres c distribution: the southern Chilterns, south Wiltshire north Dorset, east anc west Hampshire, Surrey east Sussex and east Ken There are reserves for thi species in all these area: Reliable sites include Aston Rowant NNF Oxfordshire and Martir Down NNR, Hampshire

OBSERVATION TIPS

Best looked for on ho days in late Augus

Large Skipper

Ochlodes venata

Common Resident

Wingspan: male 29–34 mr
female 31–36 mr
Chrysalis: 19 mr
Caterpillar: 28 mr
Egg: 0·8 mm (h

This 'golden' skipper is widespread throughout much of England and Wales, where it is common in rough grassland. It is extending its range northwards.

IDENTIFICATION

ADULT : Though it is somewhat larger than both the Essex and Small Skipper, size is not the easiest identification feature. Look instead for the faint chequered pattern on both sides of the wings. The male can be told readily from the female by the prominent dark line (sex brand) on the forewing.

CHRYSALIS : Dark, but dusted with a white, waxy powder

CATERPILLAR : Bluish-green, with a dark line along the back and a yellowish line along the flank. The caterpillar folds a grass blade within which it lives **Ct** , venturing out only if necessary to feed.

EGG : Dome-shaped, pale green, laid singly on the underside of a grass blade Cock's-foot is the favoured foodplant.

BEHAVIOUR

Only active in hot weather. From about 10 am until noon the male patrols his territory in search of receptive females. The afternoon is generally spent basking in the sun. Favoured perches are often on leaves, usually close to the ground. From here, males are well positioned to launch fierce but brief attacks on rival males, or to intercept any passing female. Females are much less obtrusive and, once mated, spend most of their time resting, being active only when egg-laying or feeding.

HABITAT

As long as its requirement for tall, uncut long grasses can be met, this species is happy in a wide variety of habitats. These range from woodland rides and rough grassland to roadside verges and hedgerows, whilst it also inhabits urban parks and churchyards.

POPULATION AND CONSERVATION

The northward extension of range in recent years indicates a healthy population. However, intensive agriculture has led to the loss of many colonies. The Large Skipper depends on uncut grasses, something to be taken into account when managing its habitat.

WHERE TO FIND

An easy species to find i the right habitat anywhere in England, north to jus over the Scottish borde and throughout Wales, bu absent from most islands

OBSERVATION TIP

Best looked for on ho days, when it is mos active. It is at its mos numerous in mid-Jul

Dingy Skipper

Erynnis tages

This beautifully camouflaged species has a highly localised distribution in Britain, and has declined seriously in recent years. It is the only skipper found in Ireland.

IDENTIFICATION

ADULT : No British butterfly looks more like a moth than this. The sexes are very similar, with brown wings that can cause confusion with the Mother Shipton and Burnet Companion moths, and also the Grizzled Skipper (*page 44*). The latter differs by having an obvious pattern of black and white squares on its wings. As Dingy Skippers age, they lose wing scales and become both duller and paler **Mw** and **Fw** .

CHRYSALIS : Brown, formed in early April, with the adult emerging a month later.

CATERPILLAR : Green, with a dark green line along back and distinctive dark head.

EGG : Green, soon turning orange, and laid singly on leaves of Common Bird's-foot-trefoil, its preferred foodplant.

BEHAVIOUR

Much of the day is spent basking with wings wide open on bare patches of ground, where they can be easily overlooked. Both sexes are fast fliers, the males chasing passing females, sometimes towering high into the sky. A roosting Dingy Skipper looks most moth-like because of its curious way of perching with its wings curved in a manner unlike any other British butterfly.

HABITAT

A butterfly that favours a variety of open sunny habitats, being found on chalk downland, heathland, railway lines, disused quarries and waste ground. It favours areas of bare earth, plus taller vegetation for roosting.

POPULATION AND CONSERVATION

A worrying decline in recent years seems to be almost entirely due to loss of habitat. Management of habitat by techniques such as extensive grazing and scrub clearance has been shown to help this disappearing species. Many sites in the Midlands rely on the protection of post-industrial 'brownfield' sites.

Localised Resident	
Wingspan:	27–34 m
Chrysalis:	14 m
Caterpillar:	17 m
Egg:	0·5 (w) x 0·5 mm (

WHERE TO FIND

Most easily seen on i
southern strongholds: th
downs of Hampshire
Dorset and Wiltshire
Magdalen Hill Dowr
Hampshire, is a reliabl
site. In Ireland, the Burre
is a favoured localit

OBSERVATION TIP

Look for this butterfly o
warm, south-facing slope
Peak emergence is in lat
Ma

Grizzled Skipper

Pyrgus malvae

Declining Resident	
Wingspan:	23–29 m
Chrysalis:	13 m
Caterpillar:	18 m
Egg:	0·6 (w) x 0·5 mm (

This skipper is a spring butterfly, found most commonly on our southern chalk downlands. It is a declining species throughout much of its range.

IDENTIFICATION

ADULT : Tiny and rather moth-like, it is readily identified by its pattern of white chequers on dark wings, with distinctive black and white fringes. Male and female are very similar in appearance.

CHRYSALIS : Protected by a tent of silk, and formed near the ground.

CATERPILLAR : Green, suffused with dark brown on the back, and a large, black head.

EGG : Pale, laid singly on the foodplant, which includes a variety of species in the rose family, preferring Agrimony, Creeping Cinquefoil and Wild Strawberry.

BEHAVIOUR

This species has the typical, rapid flight of the skippers, but it is one of the most accomplished fliers; battles between rival males include spectacular displays of flying skills. Males like to bask in the sun in favoured sheltered hollows, every now and again darting off at speed to attack a rival or court a female. Typically lives in small, self-contained colonies.

HABITAT

Though usually thought of as a butterfly of chalk downland, can also be found in a wide variety of other sites, from woodland rides and waste ground to railway lines. The chief requirement appears to be a plentiful supply of foodplants, patches of bare ground, and an abundance of spring nectar plants.

POPULATION AND CONSERVATION

A declining species that has suffered from an increasing loss of habitat due to changing patterns of land use. Populations will respond to management, such as coppicing or suitable grazing.

WHERE TO FIND

Few really large colonie still survive, and they ar usually on nature reserve The most favoure counties are Dorse Sussex and Hampshire Bentley Station Meadow Hampshire is a good site

OBSERVATION TIPS

A spring butterfly, bes looked for on hot days i late May and early June

Swallowtail

Papilio machaon

The only British representative of the spectacular family of swallowtail butterflies. Our resident race, *britannicus*, is restricted to the fenlands of the Norfolk Broads.

IDENTIFICATION

ADULT : Unmistakable, thanks to its size, colour and shape. Continental Swallowtails occasionally occur in southern England: they are slightly larger, their markings notably paler and less intense.

CHRYSALIS : There are two distinct colour forms: brown and yellowish-green.

CATERPILLAR : Resembles a bird dropping at first, but the mature caterpillar is distinctive, with green body banded with black, and each band spotted with orange.

EGG : Spherical, shiny yellow at first, becoming dark brown with age. Laid on Milk-parsley, the exclusive foodplant of the British race.

BEHAVIOUR

Adults tend to feed in the morning and evening, attracted especially to thistles and Ragged-Robin. When feeding they often flap their wings to maintain their balance. Males spend much of their day on the wing: their flight is powerful, with distinctive flaps and glides. Courtship is spectacular, with both butterflies soaring high into the sky.

HABITAT

Our resident race is restricted to open sedge fens and reed marshes in the Norfolk Broads, where Milk-parsley grows abundantly. Migrant Continental Swallowtails are much more catholic in their choice of habitat (reflecting a variety of foodplants), but are most likely to be seen on southern downland.

POPULATION AND CONSERVATION

Thanks to habitat management within the Broads, this species is now thriving, especially on nature reserves. Global warming could well lead to Continental Swallowtails becoming established in southern England.

Localised Resident

Wingspan: male 76–83 m
female 86–93 m
Chrysalis: 28–32 m
Caterpillar: 52 m
Egg: 0·9 (w) x 0·9 mm

WHERE TO FIN
There are a number
nature reserves within t
Norfolk Broads (such
Bure Marshes NN
where the habitat
managed specially for t
spectacular butterfly. Lo
out for migrants along t
south coa

OBSERVATION TIF
Unlike the continen
race, *britannicus* usually h
a single brood. Numbe
tend to be highest in t
second or third week
June, when this butterfly
easy to se

Wood White

Leptidea sinapis

Our rarest white butterfly, the Wood White is found locally in England and Wales and The Burren in Ireland.

Rare Resident

Wingspan:	42 m
Chrysalis:	16 m
Caterpillar:	19 m
Egg:	1·3mm (

IDENTIFICATION

ADULT : Small and delicate, the two species of Wood White are easy to recognise thanks to their dainty appearance and characteristic slow, fluttering flight. The shape is distinctive, too: the wings are rather long and oval, the body long and slim. Wood Whites only settle with their wings closed, obscuring the distinctive black dot on the leading corner of the forewing. The two species of Wood White are identical in appearance, and can only be separated by examination of the genitalia. The first generation **1** tends to have darker markings on the underwings than the second **2** .

CHRYSALIS : Yellowish-green, and formed in tussocks of grass away from the foodplant.

CATERPILLAR : Green, with a dark line along the middle of the back and a yellow line along the flank.

EGG : Pale, cylindrical, and laid singly on the foodplant. The latter includes a variety of legumes, including Meadow Vetchling, Tufted Vetch and Common Bird's-foot-trefoil.

BEHAVIOUR

On bright days, male Wood Whites fly almost continuously, slowly patrolling in search of females. The flight is low, seldom more than a metre above the ground, and anything white will be investigated. Females spend most of their time feeding or resting. On hot days, the males will sip salts from the edge of puddles. Seldom found far from their colony.

HABITAT

In England and Wales, Wood Whites are usually found in woodland rides or clearings, though some colonies can be found on coastal undercliffs, even disused railway lines. In Ireland it seems to be confined to Hazel scrub on The Burren limestones.

POPULATION AND CONSERVATION

Wood Whites have declined seriously in England and Wales, due to loss of habitat and, in particular, the decline in coppicing and the shading of woodland rides. If habitat is managed, and open, sunny rides maintained, colonies will thrive.

WHERE TO FIN

The English strongholo are now in three region Herefordshire ar Worcestershir Northamptonshire ar Buckinghamshire; and we Somerset and Devo

OBSERVATION TIP

Though there is a secon summer brood, the sprir brood is usually muc more numerous, so ear June visits to colonies c sunny, warm days a likely to be mo productiv

Real's Wood White

Leptidea reali

Although recorded since 1903, this butterfly was only recognised as a species in its own right in 2001, and so far has only been recorded with certainty in Ireland.

Localised Resident

Wingspan:	42 r
Chrysalis:	16 r
Caterpillar:	19 r
Egg:	1·3 mm

IDENTIFICATION

ADULT : Small and delicate, the two closely related species of Wood White can only be separated with certainty by examination of the genitalia. There do, though, appear to be subtle differences between the two species. The underside of the hindwing of Real's Wood White has a dark olive tint and there is some suggestion that the shape of the forewing tends to be rounder towards the tip. These differences are both slight and variable, however, and their reliability has not been tested. It also appears that the leg colour of Real's Wood White is whiter than that of Wood White.

CHRYSALIS / CATERPILLAR : As Wood White, although some minor differences in form and colour have been reported.

EGG : As Wood White.

BEHAVIOUR

Obervations of Real's Wood White suggest that it has a somewhat stronger, albeit still slow and ponderous flight, unlike the weak flight of Wood White. Otherwise, it exhibits the same behaviour and has the same flight period.

HABITAT

Real's Wood White seems to prefer more open habitats than Wood White, including scrubby grassland, hedges and railway lines.

POPULATION AND CONSERVATION

Real's Wood White was only identified as a separate species in Ireland in 2001. It appears to be surviving much better in Ireland than the Wood White is in England and Wales, having spread northwards along railway lines. There are, however, recent indications that its range is contracting. Due to its recent discovery, its foodplant(s) and conservation needs are not well known.

WHERE TO FIN
Real's Wood White
much more widespread
Ireland than the Woc
White (which, in Ireland,
confined to The Burren

OBSERVATION TIP
Look for its slo
ponderous flight aroun
patches of scrub or alon
hedges and verges
Ireland, away from Th
Burre

Clouded Yellow

Colias croceus

This beautiful golden-yellow butterfly is an annual migrant to Britain. Numbers vary enormously from year to year, with exceptional 'Clouded Yellow summers' typically occurring once in a decade.

IDENTIFICATION

ADULT : With its rich, chrome-yellow wings heavily edged in black, the Clouded Yellow is one of the easiest butterflies to identify. The female is normally slightly darker than the male, and her wing margins are dotted with yellow spots. Some 10% of females are of the pale variety, *helice* hel , their colour ranging from a soft lemon-yellow to white. The distinctive underwing pattern is the same as for the normal variety. The uppersides of the Clouded Yellow are illustrated on page 160.

CHRYSALIS : Green, with a pale yellow stripe on the back and black spots on the underside at the rear end.

CATERPILLAR : Green, speckled with black, and with a fine yellow line along each side.

EGG : White when first laid, turning pinkish, and laid singly on clovers, Lucerne or Common Bird's-foot-trefoil.

BEHAVIOUR

A highly migratory species that reaches our shores every year, but is only really common and widespread about once every decade. During so-called 'Clouded Yellow summers', the species is abundant, and fields of clover fill with these beautiful butterflies. They are powerful fliers, travelling fast and low, and when they pause to feed, they invariably do so with their wings closed. The breeding cycle is extremely quick: an egg laid in early June may produce an adult butterfly by mid-July.

HABITAT

As wandering migrants, Clouded Yellows can occur anywhere, but they favour chalk downlands, and are one of the few butterflies that like extensive fields of clover and Lucerne.

POPULATION AND CONSERVATION

The size of the British population depends entirely on the number that migrate here, as this species finds the British winter too cold and wet for over-wintering. In a Clouded Yellow summer, the population can be measured in millions, while in a poor year it may just be hundreds.

Annual Migrant

Wingspan:	male 52–58 m
	female 54–62 m
Chrysalis:	22 m
Caterpillar:	33 m
Egg:	1·1 mm

WHERE TO FIN
In a good year, anywhere but especially fields c clover. In a poor year, th South Downs are th most likely place to se this specie

OBSERVATION TIP
The sight of hug numbers of Cloude Yellows migrating north one of the wonders c nature, but a rare treat fo British observer

Brimstone

Gonepteryx rhamni

The Brimstone is the original 'butter-coloured fly'. This species is steadily extending its range northwards.

Widespread Resident	
Wingspan:	60–74 n
Chrysalis:	22–24 n
Caterpillar:	32–34 n
Egg:	1·3 mm

IDENTIFICATION

ADULT : A male Brimstone is difficult to confuse with any other British butterfly thanks to its sulphur-yellow wings. The wandering flight is usually high and conspicuous, and totally unlike the fast, low flight of a Clouded Yellow, our only other yellow butterfly. In contrast, the female is a very pale lemon yellow, and can, at a distance, be confused with a Large White, but she has no black on the wings. When perched, the distinctive leaf-like wing shape of both sexes is diagnostic.

CHRYSALIS : Shaped and coloured to resemble a leaf.

CATERPILLAR : Green, finely speckled with black, and with a white spiracular line.

EGG : Pale yellow, and lozenge-shaped, laid on the underside of the leaves of Buckthorn or Alder Buckthorn.

BEHAVIOUR

Warm, sunny days in early March rouse Brimstones from their hibernation: patrolling males are usually one of the first signs of spring. Though there is only one generation of Brimstones a year, this is such a long-lived species that adults may be seen on the wing in almost every month. Mating takes place only in the spring, when the spiralling courtship flight is a familiar sight. Brimstones always shut their wings when resting or feeding.

HABITAT

Brimstones favour scrubby woodland and hedgerows where their foodplants grow.

POPULATION AND CONSERVATION

The Brimstone's range in Britain is limited by the availability of its foodplants. However, its range has been extending northwards in recent years, though the overall population has probably fallen in line with the destruction of hedgerows during the second half of the 20th century.

WHERE TO FIN

A great wanderer, so c
be found alm(
anywhere within its ran;

OBSERVATION TI

Look out for this spec
on the first warm days
spri

Large White

Pieris brassicae

Our largest white butterfly, and the one most disliked by gardeners, who usually refer to it as the Cabbage White. Numbers vary from year to year, depending partly on migration from the continent.

Common Resident

Wingspan:	male 58 m
	female 63 m
Chrysalis:	20 m
Caterpillar:	45 m
Egg:	1·4mm

IDENTIFICATION

ADULT : Our largest white butterfly. The female in particular is a handsome insect, with conspicuous black double dots on the forewings, and a pale yellow wash to the upperside of the hindwing. Both sexes have a similar underside. Though typically bigger than the Small White (*page 58*), there can be an overlap with runt specimens of this species, but the black tips to the wings are always much more extensive on the Large White. The second generation of the Large White **2** has stronger black markings than those of the first generation **1** .

CHRYSALIS : Speckled, but the pattern is variable.

CATERPILLAR : The pale green body is heavily spotted with black on the back, with a yellow line along the middle of the back and a band of pale yellow along the spiracles.

EGG : Cylinder-shaped with ridges; pale yellow, becoming orange, and laid in clusters on wild or cultivated species of the Cruciferae family, and in particular Cabbage.

BEHAVIOUR

Our resident population is reinforced annually with migrants from the Continent. Migrating Large Whites can travel at up to 10mph given favourable wind conditions, but once settled in an area their flight is typically much more relaxed.

HABITAT

A widespread and adaptable butterfly that occurs as far north as Shetland. Though it can be encountered almost anywhere, it particularly likes gardens and allotments where Cabbages and Brussels-sprouts are grown.

POPULATION AND CONSERVATION

A highly successful and flourishing species, though numbers fluctuate due to parasitism of caterpillars by tiny wasps. Regarded as a pest by many gardeners.

WHERE TO FIN
Almost anywher

OBSERVATION TIP
Look out for migra
Large Whites headi
north in the sprir

Small White

Pieris rapae

A highly successful species that is common throughout Britain and Ireland. It is equally widespread throughout Europe, occurs as far east as Japan, and has become established in both North America and Australia.

IDENTIFICATION

ADULT : Similar in appearance to the Large White (*page 56*), but usually noticeably smaller. The black on the wing tips is much less extensive than on the Large White, and that of first brood males is often faint. Females are always darker than males and have two distinct spots on the upperside of the forewing. The male has one – a feature the male Large White lacks. The second brood **2** has darker markings than the first **1**. Can also be confused with the Green-veined White (*page 60*), but the underwings of the Small White lack any green markings along the veins.

CHRYSALIS : Variable in colour, from bright green to earth-brown, depending on the background against which it forms. Supported by a silken girdle and thread and found in a variety of locations, such as on fences, walls and trees. The spring generation tends to produce a higher proportion of green chrysali in July; the summer generation chrysali overwinter.

CATERPILLAR : Head green, speckled with black, body velvety, blue-green with a thin yellow line down the back

EGG : Conical in shape, straw-coloured at first, turning yellow then brownish-grey. Laid singly on the underside of a foodplant in a sheltered position.

BEHAVIOUR

A common and familiar butterfly. The resident population is boosted every year by influxes of migrants from the Continent. Many of these will find their way into gardens, whey they are attracted by white flowers, from which they sip nectar, and cultivated brassicas and Nasturtium on which they lay their eggs.

HABITAT

Almost anywhere, but gardens are particularly popular, as are fields of Oil-seed Rape.

POPULATION AND CONSERVATION

A highly successful species that continues to flourish in 21st century Britain.

Abundant Resident	
Wingspan:	38–57 mm
Chrysalis:	19 mm
Caterpillar:	25 mm
Egg:	1·0mm (h

WHERE TO FIND
Almost anywhere, bu
does not occur as fa
north as Large White

OBSERVATION TIPS
Be wary of the occasiona
overlap in size betweer
this species and the Large
White

58

F1

F1

M1

F2

M2

Ca

Ch

M2

Green-veined White

Pieris napi

One of our most widespread butterflies, found throughout Britain apart from Shetland. It is usually the commonest white butterfly in northern Britain, and occurs at higher altitudes than the other species.

IDENTIFICATION

ADULT : Though often mistaken for the Small White (*page 58*), closer inspection reveals a delicate, attractive butterfly, with conspicuous dark veins on the upperside of the wings, and the same veins on the underside etched in green on a pale yellow background. A very variable butterfly depending on location and season. Females are more heavily marked than males. First brood butterflies ➊ are smaller than their offspring ➋, and the males may be almost white.

CHRYSALIS : Two colour forms: green and pale brown.

CATERPILLAR : Green; similar to Small White but lacks the yellow line along the back.

EGG : Elongated, pale green, laid singly on a range of wild crucifers, including Garlic Mustard, Charlock, Hedge Mustard and Cuckooflower.

BEHAVIOUR

A wide-ranging species with a rather fluttery flight. Both sexes spend a great deal of time feeding, while males not uncommonly suck minerals from the edge of muddy puddles. This is often an abundant butterfly and adults can be seen on the wing from early April through to early September.

HABITAT

An adaptable species found in a wide variety of habitats from hedgerows to riverbanks. Damp, lush vegetation is an essential requirement.

POPULATION AND CONSERVATION

One of the world's most successful butterflies, and one that continues to do well in Britain. This species is likely to benefit from the trend towards warmer summers, unless these summers also become drier since drought conditions invariably lead to a fall in numbers.

Common Resident

Wingspan:	40–52 mm
Chrysalis:	19 mm
Caterpillar:	25 mm
Egg:	1·0 mm (h)

WHERE TO FIND
Almost anywhere in Britain and Ireland, but absent from Shetland

OBSERVATION TIPS
Look out for local variations in colour: Irish and Scottish butterflies have stronger markings and brighter yellow underwings

60

Orange-tip

Anthocharis cardamines

No butterfly better symbolises the arrival of spring than this delightfully delicate species. It is currently extending its range northwards, and is now well established in much of Scotland.

IDENTIFICATION

ADULT : A male Orange-tip is unmistakable, thanks to his bright orange-tipped wings, but the female is similar in appearance – if not shape and jizz – to other whites. However, when perched she is readily identifiable by the beautiful green mottling of the underside of the hindwing.

CHRYSALIS : Two colour forms: the brown is more common than the green.

CATERPILLAR : Greenish-grey on the back, fading to white on the flanks.

EGG : Long and thin, pale green when first laid, turning orange with age. Laid singly on the flower-heads of a variety of plants, but most commonly Cuckooflower and Garlic Mustard.

BEHAVIOUR

In the south of its range this is a wandering species that seldom pauses for long anywhere, but never seems to be in much of a hurry. A wandering male certainly covers an extensive area. In the north, this butterfly is apparently far more sedentary, living in colonies and seldom ranging far.

HABITAT

Damp, grassy habitats are preferred, including roadside verges, meadows and grassy woodland glades. In the north, colonies are usually found in wetter habitats where Cuckooflower grows commonly.

POPULATION AND CONSERVATION

Though this species may be extending its range northwards, it is generally thought to be much less common in the south than formerly. The switch from hay- to silage-making, drainage of wet meadows and the general intensification of agriculture has caused widespread loss of its favoured habitats.

Widespread Resident	
Wingspan:	40–52 mm
Chrysalis:	23 m
Caterpillar:	31 m
Egg:	1·2 mm (

WHERE TO FIN
Most easily found
countryside where
mosaic of hedgerow
small woodlands ar
meadows remai

OBSERVATION TIP
One of the first butterfli
to look out for in th
spring, but numbe
decline rapidly in th
south as June progresse
The flight period is a litt
later in the north. A
unusually early seaso
may lead to a sm
second brood in th
summe

Green Hairstreak

Callophrys rubi

Widespread Resident

Wingspan:	27–34 m
Chrysalis:	8–9.5 m
Caterpillar:	16–18 m
Egg:	0.65 mm (v

Like all the hairstreaks, the Green is easily overlooked, despite occurring in a wide variety of habitats. It is still widespread, but habitat destruction during recent decades has led to the loss of many colonies.

IDENTIFICATION

ADULT: Unmistakable, as this is the only British butterfly with a green underside to the wings. The upperside is a plain and unmarked brown, though the larger female is generally paler than the male. The male does, however, display a light scent patch or sex brand on the forewing.

CHRYSALIS: Brown, hairy, and formed underground, possibly in an ants' nest.

CATERPILLAR: Green with yellow markings, and strongly indented between the segments.

EGG: The white eggs are laid on a wide variety of foodplants, including Common Bird's-foot-trefoil and Common Rock-rose, on chalk downland; Gorse and Broom on moorland and Bilberry in Scotland.

BEHAVIOUR

Territorial males have favourite perches on prominent shrubs, from which they launch periodic attacks on intruding males or chase passing females, usually returning to the same perch afterwards. When perched, always with wings closed, they are usually tame and approachable. Females are most likely to be seen when egg-laying.

HABITAT

Found on a wide variety of soils, and in a range of habitats including woodland rides, heathland, moorland and chalk downland. Its chief requirements are open grassland or moorland with patches of scrub.

POPULATION AND CONSERVATION

Still widespread, but many colonies have been lost through habitat destruction or deterioration; overgrazing and afforestation having led to losses in upland habitats. The Green Hairstreak requires extensive grazing and sensitive scrub management.

WHERE TO FIN

Warm, sheltered sites wi
plenty of scrub on cha
downland, heathland
moorland. This is the mo
widespread hairstre
occurring in Britain ar
Irelar

OBSERVATION TIP

A much overlook
species, partially becau
of its early flight perio
Tapping likely looki
bushes in suitable habi
in early June is likely
flush perching males, a
is a good way to loca
this butter

64

Brown Hairstreak

Thecla betulae

Localised Resident

Wingspan: male 36–41 m
female 39–45 m
Chrysalis: 12 m
Caterpillar: 18 m
Egg: 0·6 (w) × 0·7 mm

Over-zealous management and the destruction of hedgerows has hastened the decline of this handsome hairstreak. Its current range is highly localised.

IDENTIFICATION

ADULT : The biggest and darkest of our hairstreaks (notably darker than the Black). Both sexes have dark chocolate-brown wings with orange tails, but the larger female also has a bright band of golden-orange across the forewings. The underside is a contrasting orange-yellow, more intense on the female, with white lines across both wings. If seen well, identification is easy.

CHRYSALIS : Formed on the ground at the base of a clump of grass, in a crevice or on a leaf, and is attractive to ants.

CATERPILLAR : Greenish, strongly indented between segments.

EGG : White, and laid singly on young twigs of Blackthorn, the foodplant.

BEHAVIOUR

This butterfly is one of our most elusive, as it spends most of its life out of sight, either high in the tree canopy or tucked away in hedgerows. As a result it is probably our least observed butterfly. Like the Purple Emperor, males of this species apparently use a 'master tree', normally an Ash, which stands above the surrounding tree canopy. Here they congregate, along with unmated females after they emerge. Males only rarely descend to feed, but when they do they are tame and approachable. Females are more often seen, as they disperse to lay their eggs, but they are only active on sunny days when the temperature is above 20°C.

HABITAT

Usually found in hedgerows, scrub and woodland edge, with abundant Blackthorn, on heavy clay soils. Irish colonies are found on lighter, limestone soils.

POPULATION AND CONSERVATION

Hedgerow destruction and modern hedgerow management practices have led to a considerable decline in the distribution of this butterfly. Annual hedge-trimming by tractor-mounted mechanical flails destroys eggs. Conservation is difficult because a single colony breeds over a wide area. Encouraging a reduction in the frequency of hedge-trimming and the retention of abundant woodland is the best conservation measure.

WHERE TO FIN

The west Weald in We
Sussex and Surrey,
sheltered and low-lyi
valleys in north Devc
south-west Somerset, a
in south-west Wales.
Ireland, The Burren is t
best place to loc

OBSERVATION TII

One of the hardest Brit
species to see; eggs a
easier to find than adu
Always take binocul
and look out for t
golden females in l
summ

Purple Hairstreak

Neozephyrus quercus

This beautiful butterfly is surprisingly widespread and often quite numerous; it is possibly the most abundant British hairstreak, but easily overlooked.

Widespread Resident

Wingspan: male 33–40 m
female 31–38 m
Chrysalis: 10 m
Caterpillar: 16 m
Egg: 0·8 (w) × 0·5 mm (

IDENTIFICATION

ADULT : No other butterfly of this size shares the same attractive colouring. The male's black-edged wings are sheened with purple, but the female only has a flash of purple on the forewing. The underwing of both sexes is similar, with prominent white lines on a greyish background, and orange-yellow spots near the corner of the hindwing.

CHRYSALIS : Dark-brown, and formed underground, probably in an ants' nest.

CATERPILLAR : Reddish-brown, and well camouflaged.

EGG : White, spherical, and laid in ones or twos on the tips of oak branches, adjacent to the following year's buds.

BEHAVIOUR

Purple Hairstreaks live in self-contained colonies, always on oak trees. They seldom take flight, except on sunny days, when they can be seen flying around the tree-tops, only occasionally descending to lower branches. Individuals often congregate in the late afternoon and early evening on bright, sunny days. When seen in flight from below, they appear silver. Unlike our other hairstreaks, they bask with their wings open.

HABITAT

Oak trees in mature woodlands, parklands and hedgerows; sometimes in scrub oak on heathland. Even single, isolated trees may support a colony.

POPULATION AND CONSERVATION

Recent increases in range indicate a healthy population, even though many colonies were lost during the last century. However, the future looks bright for this species in England and Wales, if not in Ireland, where it has always been very rare.

WHERE TO FIN

Check suitable habi
with oak trees anywhe
within range; this is one
the most overlooked
our butterfli

OBSERVATION TIF

Best looked for in the la
afternoon or early eveni
on bright sunny days, a
with the aid of binocula
The flight period exten
throughout Augu

White-letter Hairstreak

Satyrium w-album

Dutch Elm Disease dealt a savage blow to this elm-dependent butterfly, but it will happily breed on the more resistant Wych Elm, and on elm suckers.

IDENTIFICATION

ADULT : Look for the distinctive white letter W on the underside. Most easily confused with the Black Hairstreak, but paler on the underside and it lacks the latter's orange spots on the upper hindwing. The upperwings are darker than the Black Hairstreak (*page 72*), but, as it never settles with its wings open, this is invariably impossible to see.

CHRYSALIS : Brown and hairy, closely resembling an elm bud.

CATERPILLAR : Green, and well camouflaged as they feed on elm leaves.

EGG : Flying-saucer shaped, and laid on elm twigs.

BEHAVIOUR

Like other hairstreaks, this species has an erratic, spiralling flight, and spends much of its time high in the tree canopy. They will, however, occasionally take nectar from nearby flowers, favouring Creeping Thistle and Bramble.

HABITAT

Requires elm trees, and usually found in sheltered hedgerows where elm suckers grow well. Can also be found on isolated, mature elm trees where these remain.

POPULATION AND CONSERVATION

Dependent upon elms, but has managed to overcome the problems caused by Dutch Elm Disease by breeding on elm suckers (the shoots of elm that grow from the rootstock). After a decline in the 1970s, it appears to have made a good recovery and is now abundant in some areas. Due to is behaviour, the White-letter Hairstreak is, however, easily overlooked.

Widespread Resident

Wingspan: male 25–35 m
female 26–36 m
Chrysalis: 9 m
Caterpillar: 16 m
Egg: 0·8 (w) × 0·4 mm (

WHERE TO FIN

Wherever there are elm
in southern and centr
England. Northward H
RSPB reserve in Kent ar
Narborough Railway Lin
Norfolk, are reliable site

OBSERVATION TIP

As with most hairstreak
the adults are both high,
elusive and difficult to se
as they normally rema
high in the canopy. The
will take nectar early
the morning or late in th
afternoon. Best looked fo
in the first three weeks o
Ju

Black Hairstreak

Satyrium pruni

With just 45 colonies, all in the East Midlands, this is one of our rarest and most elusive butterflies.

Localised Resident

Wingspan: male 34–39 m
female 35–40 m
Chrysalis: 9·5 m
Caterpillar: 16 m
Egg: 0·8 (w) × 0·4 mm (

IDENTIFICATION

ADULT : Seen from below – the most usual view – it is easily confused with both Purple (*page 68*) and White-letter Hairstreaks (*page 70*); all three species fly at the same time of the year and in the same habitat. The feature to look for is the row of black spots in the outer orange margin of the hindwing. This distinguishes both sexes with certainty, but binoculars might be needed to see it. Unlike the Purple Hairstreak, but like the White-letter, this species never basks with its wings open. Its name is misleading, for its forewings are a dark golden-brown, rather than black; they have orange markings, which are more extensive in the female than the male.

CHRYSALIS : Attached to a twig, and resembling a bird dropping.

CATERPILLAR : Changes colour with age, becoming bright leaf green.

EGG : Sea-urchin shaped, laid on Blackthorn twigs, where they remain for nine months before hatching.

BEHAVIOUR

Highly elusive, sometimes hardly flying at all, but simply sitting out of sight on the tops of Ash or Field Maple trees, feeding on aphid honeydew. When they do fly, their flight is characteristically jerky, and very similar to both Purple and White-letter Hairstreaks. They will occasionally come down to the ground, where they are attracted to the flowers of Dog-rose and Wild Privet. When feeding or basking they are often tame and easy to approach closely.

HABITAT

Typically, mature and dense stands of Blackthorn in sheltered and sunny positions, but may also occur along sheltered hedgerows or in small patches of scrub.

POPULATION AND CONSERVATION

The population has declined steadily during the 20th century, mainly due to the clearance of Blackthorn. The majority of colonies are now on nature reserves where the habitat can be managed for them.

WHERE TO FINI

Restricted exclusively an mysteriously to woodland on heavy clay soils in th East Midlands, betwee Oxford and Peterborougr Monks Wood NNF Cambridgeshire, is a classi site, as is Glapthorn Co\ Pastures, Northant‹

OBSERVATION TIP!

Difficult to find, even ã known colonies. The fligh period is short: the bes time to find this species the last week of June an‹ the first week of July. Tak binocular‹

Small Copper

Lycaena phlaeas

A common and widespread species, but one that underwent a major decline in abundance during the 20th century.

IDENTIFICATION

ADULT: Readily identified by its bright burnished copper forewings, with black margins and spots. The hindwings are dark with black-spotted copper margins. No other British butterfly shares the same colouring. The female is larger than the male and has less pointed forewings. This species is prone to variation, and albinos are regularly recorded.

CHRYSALIS: For such a common butterfly it is surprising how little is known about this stage of its life-cycle. Rarely found in the wild, it is thought to be tended by ants amongst leaf litter.

CATERPILLAR: Sometimes plain green, but often with a purple line along the back.

EGG: Laid singly on Common Sorrel or Sheep's Sorrel.

BEHAVIOUR

Males are highly territorial, attacking with pugnacious enthusiasm any insect that comes close. The flight is both fast and direct. After a quick sortie he usually returns to his perch, typically on a flower-head that gives good all-round visibility. A highly active insect, fidgeting even when feeding.

HABITAT

Its widespread distribution reflects its use of a variety of habitats, ranging from heathland and unimproved grassland to woodland clearings. Often found on waste ground, churchyards and occasionally in gardens. The Small Copper is particularly fond of warm and dry situations.

POPULATION AND CONSERVATION

Population declines have been caused by intensive agriculture, as it cannot survive on fertilised grass swards. Much still needs to be discovered about its ecology, but it is known to suffer badly during cool, wet summers.

Common Resident

Wingspan: male 26–36 m
female 30–40 m
Chrysalis: 10·5 m
Caterpillar: 16 m
Egg: 0·6 (w) × 0·3 mm (

WHERE TO FIN
Almost anywhere, b
look for it particularly c
waste ground or margin
land where sorre
flouris

OBSERVATION TIP
Easy to find and high
entertaining to watch. Ca
be seen from early M
through to mid-Octobe

Small Blue

Cupido minimus

Our smallest butterfly. It is patchily distributed throughout Britain and is declining in most areas.

Declining Resident

Wingspan:	18–27 m
Chrysalis:	8 m
Caterpillar:	9·5 m
Egg:	0·45 (w) × 0·2 mm (

IDENTIFICATION

ADULT : Readily identified with practice thanks to its small size, dainty appearance and rounded wings with silvery-blue undersides. These are dotted with black, with none of the orange found on most blues. It resembles a tiny Holly Blue (*page 90*). Though the underside of both sexes is similar, the female lacks any hint of blue in her upperwings, while the male shows a distinct scatter of blue scales at the base of the wings. The flight is weak and fluttery.

CHRYSALIS : Pale sepia, with brown dots.

CATERPILLAR : Pale yellow, with a dark line down the back, and a whitish line along each side.

EGG : Tiny, disc-shaped and white. They are laid within the flower head of the sole foodplant, Kidney Vetch.

BEHAVIOUR

A colonial species that is usually highly sedentary, but does occasionally disperse to new sites. Males can typically be found basking together in a sheltered south-facing site, usually at the base of a hill, quarry slope or railway embankment. Here they spend most of the day perched up to a metre or so above the ground, and spaced up to a couple of metres apart, with wings held partially open towards the sun. Any passing female is quickly courted and mated by a waiting male; she then spends her time on patches of Kidney Vetch, where she not only rests and feeds, but also lays her eggs.

HABITAT

Small Blues favour sheltered grassland, usually on chalk or limestone, where Kidney Vetch grows in abundance. They like a mixture of short turf and taller, scrubby vegetation.

POPULATION AND CONSERVATION

Its special requirements of shelter and abundance of Kidney Vetch limit the number of sites where it can be found, while habitat loss during the past century has led to the extinction of many colonies. The increasing isolation of many populations and the lack of suitable site management are major threats to its survival, and explains why this species is in worrying decline.

WHERE TO FIN
Though it occurs fror
Caithness to Dorset, i
strongholds are th
Cotswolds and downlar
on Salisbury Plai

OBSERVATION TIP
This is a spring butterf
best looked for in ear
June when numbers pea
There is a small secon
brood in the sout

Silver-studded Blue

Plebeius argus

A localised butterfly of heathland. Many colonies have been lost during the last century, but it is often abundant where it still occurs.

Localised Resident

Wingspan: male 26–32 m
female 25–31 m
Chrysalis: 8–9 m
Caterpillar: 13 m
Egg: 0·6 (d) × 0·3 mm

IDENTIFICATION

ADULT : An extremely variable species. The male is best told from the similar Common Blue (*page 84*) by the thick black borders to both the underwing and upperwing. With practice it is possible to tell the two apart by colour – the Silver-studded is generally described as lead-blue. The brown females are a challenge: look for the blue centres to the black spots along the outer edge of the underwing. Both sexes of the Silver-studded Blue lack a black spot on the underside of the forewing close to the body which is a feature of Adonis, Common and Chalkhill Blues.

CHRYSALIS : Green, and formed underground in an ants' nest.

CATERPILLAR : Green, with a blackish stripe along the back, and a white stripe along each side.

EGG : White, disc-like, and usually laid near nests of the black ants *Lasius niger* and *L. alienus*. The foodplants include Heather, Bell Heather and Cross-leaved Heath, and also Common Bird's-foot-trefoil, Horseshoe Vetch and Common Rock-rose.

BEHAVIOUR

Flight is typically ground-hugging, slow and fluttering; individuals rarely move more than 20 m from where they emerged. The males are very active on sunny days, patrolling continuously in search of unmated females. Colonies can number hundreds or even thousands of individuals, and communal roosting involving scores or even hundreds of butterflies is normal. This butterfly has an extremely close relationship with black ants: the ants attend the caterpillars, receiving sugar-rich secretions in return.

HABITAT

Lowland heathland is the typical habitat, but this species also occurs on limestone grasslands and sand dunes. Short vegetation, and a thriving black ant population are the main requirements.

POPULATION AND CONSERVATION

The widespread fragmentation and loss of lowland heathland has led to the extinction of many colonies, while many downland populations disappeared following myxomatosis in the 1950s. Habitat management is essential for survival of the remaining colonies, either grazing or periodic, patchy burning.

WHERE TO FIN

Most lowland heathlanc in Hampshire and Dorse have flourishing colonie while classic sites incluc Great Ormes Head i north Wales, and the Is of Portland in Dorse

OBSERVATION TIP:

The Great Orme population, in which th female is largely blu rather than brown **Fgo** emerges two to thre weeks earlier than othe colonies, in late June Other populations peak i mid-Jul

Brown Argus

Aricia agestis

Confusingly, this blue butterfly is always brown. It is found on chalk and limestone, but a recent growth in numbers seems to have faltered.

Widespread Resident

Wingspan: 25–31 m
Chrysalis: 8 m
Caterpillar: 11 m
Egg: 0·5 (w) × 0·3 mm

IDENTIFICATION

ADULT : A challenging species to identify, due to its close resemblance to the brown form of the female Common Blue (*page 84*). The most reliable characteristic is the silvery appearance of both sexes when in flight, caused by the reflection of light on the underwing. One consistent feature to look for is the complete absence of blue at the base of the upperwings (female Common Blues usually show a hint of blue). In addition (and unlike Common, Adonis and Chalkhill Blues), the underside of the forewing lacks spots on the part of the wing close to the body.

CHRYSALIS : Pale pinkish-green, and formed on the ground at the base of the foodplant.

CATERPILLAR : Green, with a purplish-green stripe along the back and along the sides.

EGG : A pale, blue-green disc, laid on the underside of leaves of its foodplant, Common Rock-rose. Various other foodplants are also used, especially species of crane's-bill.

BEHAVIOUR

A colonial species, though most colonies are fairly small. At first light, adults bask together in the sun, wings stretched wide to absorb the maximum energy. A low-flying species, stopping frequently either to sip nectar from a flower, or to bask in the sun. Males frequently land on the ground. As with other blues, the caterpillars have a strong relationship with ants.

HABITAT

Traditionally found on chalk and limestone grassland, but quite adaptable and may also occur in a wide variety of other situations, including heathland, coastal dunes, woodland clearings and road verges.

POPULATION AND CONSERVATION

After a century of decline due to habitat loss, there was a resurgence in the population in the 1990s, with many new colonies being established in alternative habitats, including set-aside fields. A series of warm summers may have also played an important part in this expansion, which now seems to be faltering.

WHERE TO FIN

Though widespread
south-eastern England, th
most reliable sites to se
this species are on cha
downland in the souther
counties and th
Cotswol

OBSERVATION TIP

Thanks to two brood
and emergence over
prolonged period, th
butterfly can be seen
summer long, althoug
early June and ear
August are usually th
best times to loo

Northern Brown Argus

Aricia artaxerxes

As its name suggests, this is a northern species, widespread in Scandinavia. It can be found in small and scattered colonies: those in northern England have suffered marked declines in recent years.

IDENTIFICATION

ADULT : Very closely related to the Brown Argus (*page 80*), and most reliably separated by range. The Northern Brown Argus has a single brood, the Brown Argus has two, although the Brown Argus colonies of the Peak District and North Wales are also usually single-brooded. Until recently, these populations were thought to be of Northern Brown Argus.

Scottish populations of Northern Brown Argus are of the race *artaxerxes* **at** , where both sexes have a distinctive white spot in the middle of the forewing. This is absent in the populations of northern England, known as *salmacis* **sa** . Both sexes of Northern Brown Argus have much fainter spots on their undersides than the Brown Argus.

CHRYSALIS : Pale green, not as pink as Brown Argus.

CATERPILLAR : Similar to Brown Argus: green, with a purplish-green stripe along the back and along the sides.

EGG : A pale, blue-green disc laid, in contrast to the Brown Argus, on the upperside of its foodplant, Common Rock-rose.

BEHAVIOUR

A highly sedentary species, invariably found in small colonies of fewer than 200 adults. Its general behaviour is very similar to that of its southern counterpart, with a similar association with ants.

HABITAT

Sheltered and well-drained hillsides, usually on limestone, where its foodplant, Common Rock-rose, grows commonly. In Scotland it may also occur on acidic soils. It favours areas of bare ground within its colonies.

POPULATION AND CONSERVATION

Declined in recent years in northern England, but still relatively plentiful within its Scottish range. Fragmentation and destruction of habitat has led to loss of many colonies, and it requires light grazing from rabbits, sheep or cattle to keep conditions suitable. This species responds quickly to habitat management, with light autumn and winter grazing preferred.

Localised Resident

Wingspan:	26–35 m
Chrysalis:	8·5 m
Caterpillar:	12 m
Egg:	0·6 (w) × 0·3 mm

WHERE TO FIN

In England, Castle Ed Dene in Northumberlar the limestone outcrops south Cumbria and nor Lancashire. In Scotlar best looked for in nor Tayside and Perthshire, b there may be oth colonies to be discovere

OBSERVATION TIP

Flight period vari considerably each year ar from colony to colo Most colonies peak numbers from late June early July, often weeks lat in northern Scotlar

82

Common Blue
Polyommatus icarus

By far our most widespread blue butterfly. Though it has suffered some local declines, it remains a common species throughout much of Britain.

Common Resident

Wingspan:	29–36 m
Chrysalis:	9–10 m
Caterpillar:	13 m
Egg:	0·5 mm (

IDENTIFICATION
ADULT : The male is a brilliant, eye-catching blue, but the females are usually brown, with a touch of blue near the wing base. However, females in Ireland and north-west Scotland are blue, with the wing margins edged with orange spots and are considered to be a separate race *mariscolore* Fm . Both species have orange marks on the edges of the underwings, and a conspicuous dark spot on the underside of the forewing near the body. Aberrant forms of the Common Blue are sometimes encountered, the form *radiata* rad is one of the more common.

CHRYSALIS : Green, and attractive to ants due to sugary secretions.

CATERPILLAR : Green body, with a dark-green line along the back and greenish-white lines along the sides.

EGG : White, and laid on tiny, tender leaves of its foodplants, which include Bird's-foot-trefoil, Common Restharrow and Black Medick.

BEHAVIOUR
Common Blues live is discrete colonies, though individuals will wander some distance away. The males are territorial, and will chase away rival males, or other butterflies (especially Small Coppers). The flight is typically short but rapid as the butterfly moves from one flower to the next. Basking with wings held flat only occurs in weak, early morning or evening sunshine.

HABITAT
Its wide distribution reflects its catholic taste in habitat, as it can be found almost anywhere its foodplants grow. It favours sunny, sheltered areas, and is often to be found on downland, road verges and golf courses and in woodland clearings and rural gardens.

POPULATION AND CONSERVATION
Though a robust and successful species, it is vulnerable to changes of land use and loss of habitat. However, it is a relatively mobile butterfly and able rapidly to colonise new areas.

WHERE TO FIN
Almost anywhere
Britain, from Orkney
the north to the Isles
Scilly in the sou

OBSERVATION TIF
The best time to watch
photograph this butter
is early or late in the d
when individuals are hig
approachable as they ba
in weak sunshir

Chalkhill Blue
Polyommatus coridon

Localised Resident	
Wingspan:	33–40 m
Chrysalis:	12 m
Caterpillar:	16 m
Egg:	0·5 (w) × 0·3 mm (

The aptly named Chalkhill Blue favours chalk downland. It is common, where unimproved chalk downland remains, but has suffered from the widespread ploughing of the downs.

IDENTIFICATION

ADULT : This species is readily identified by the male's pale, almost silvery wings, quite unlike any of our other blues. The female is dark brown, and easily confused with the slightly smaller Adonis Blue (*page 88*). The Chalkhill Blue's white-edged spots around the margins of the underside of the upperwings separate the two species. Colour variations are relatively common, including blue forms of the female.

CHRYSALIS : Sepia-green, and attracts ants.

CATERPILLAR : Green body with two yellow bands along the back and a double stripe along each side.

EGG : A robust, sculptured shell, laid on or near Horseshoe Vetch, the sole foodplant.

BEHAVIOUR

On sunny days the males flutter continuously over the turf searching for females. The latter, in contrast, seldom fly far except to feed or lay eggs. Feeding adults will visit a wide variety of flowers, but they are particularly fond of scabious, knapweeds and Kidney Vetch. In the evening, the adults roost on tall grass stems, usually at the base of a slope.

HABITAT

As the name suggests, this species requires unimproved and unfertilised grassland on chalk and limestone hills where its foodplant, Horseshoe Vetch, grows. Autumn or winter grazing by sheep or cattle creates the ideal sward.

POPULATION AND CONSERVATION

The ploughing and so-called 'improvement' of grassland on many of our southern downs has led to the loss of numerous colonies. Numbers rose generally during the warm summers of the 1990s. The key to its conservation is grazing to ensure the survival of its foodplant.

WHERE TO FIN
Colonies can be found o
the North and Sou
Downs, the Chilterns ar
the Cotswolds, and th
Hampshire, Wiltshire ar
Dorset Dowr

OBSERVATION TIP
Mid-August is the be
time for viewing th
species, when numbe
are at their peak, ar
hundreds of butterfli
may be seen at on

Adonis Blue

Polyommatus bellargus

Another chalk-dependent butterfly that has suffered from the loss of downland. Where colonies have survived, it is often abundant.

Localised Resident

Wingspan:	30–40 m
Chrysalis:	11 m
Caterpillar:	15 m
Egg:	0·5 (w) × 0·3 mm (

IDENTIFICATION

ADULT : The male is the most brightly coloured of the blues, though the colour does vary considerably. Most individuals are brilliant sky-blue, while others are more turquoise, or even violet. Some flying individuals can be confused with Common Blues, and the two species can be found together. Both sexes of Adonis Blue have fine black lines that cross the outer white fringes of the wings, a feature the Common Blue lacks. The female is usually brown (though blue females are common on some sites) and very similar to the Chalkhill Blue.

CHRYSALIS : Formed underground in association with ants.

CATERPILLAR : Dark green with yellow stripes, invariably attended by ants.

EGG : Laid singly on Horseshoe Vetch, the sole foodplant.

BEHAVIOUR

This attractive butterfly lives in highly sedentary colonies. The brilliant males are far more conspicuous than the females as they patrol slowly, just above the ground, in their quest for virgin females. Like several of the other blues, this species has a close and intriguing relationship with ants (either the black ant *Lasius alienus* or the red ant *Myrmica sabuleti*).

HABITAT

Warm, south-facing slopes on dry chalk or limestone grassland. It likes unimproved and unfertilised close-cropped turf with an abundance of its foodplant, Horseshoe Vetch.

WHERE TO FIND

On the chalk or limeston hills of southern England Classic sites includ Fontmell Down and th Purbeck Hills in Dorse

POPULATION AND CONSERVATION

Though its distribution is highly restricted, it can be found in hundreds on some sites. Recent years have seen a recovery in numbers after previous declines, almost certainly due to a resurgence in rabbit populations, and improved management to create its favoured short-turf habitat. Global warming may well lead to a continued population increase, but not if our summers become too dry, as the Adonis Blue suffers badly in drought years.

OBSERVATION TIP

Of the two broods, th second is usually the mo numerous. Visit colonies i late August in order t see large number

Holly Blue

Celastrina argiolus

Common Resident

Wingspan:	26–34 m
Chrysalis:	8–9 m
Caterpillar:	15 m
Egg:	0·6 (w) × 0·3 mm

The first of the blue butterflies on the wing, this is a widespread species which is extending its range, but one whose numbers fluctuate wildly from year to year probably due to the depredations of a parasitic wasp.

IDENTIFICATION

ADULT : Habitat and timing are good clues to identifying this butterfly. A blue butterfly, seen in April flying around Holly, is almost certainly a Holly Blue, but confusion is possible later in the year when Common Blues (*page 84*) are on the wing. A good view of the underside will confirm the species, however, for the Holly Blue has a distinctive pale blue underwing spotted lightly with black and silver, but with no trace of orange. In addition, the upperwings of the female have distinctive black margins (these are much broader in the second brood **F2**).

CHRYSALIS : Hardly ever found in the wild: sepia speckled with brown.

CATERPILLAR : Usually green or yellowish-green, but highly variable, normally with a whitish line along either side.

EGG : Resembles a tiny white disc, and laid direct onto the foodplant: Holly (first brood) or Ivy (second brood).

BEHAVIOUR

Wandering Holly Blues can often be seen be seen moving along hedgerows or through sheltered gardens, typically flying much higher than any of the other blues. In drought summers the males will often come down to take salts from muddy puddles. They typically perch with their wings closed, though will partially open their wings in weak sunshine.

HABITAT

A wide variety of habitats is used, ranging from hedgerows and woodland rides to gardens and even urban parks.

POPULATION AND CONSERVATION

Populations typically rise for a few years and then peak before crashing, probably due to the effects of depredation by the parasitic ichneumon wasp *Listrodomus nycthemerus*. This wasp injects its eggs into the living caterpillar, and the growing grub feasts on the caterpillar, which it eventually kills. However, the Holly Blue is extending its range northwards, and is a species that is flourishing in Britain. It can be encouraged easily in gardens by planting Holly and Ivy.

WHERE TO FIN
Churchyards, with the abundance of Holly ar Ivy, are often good plac to look, but larg sheltered gardens als attract this butter

OBSERVATION TIP
In an early spring, look o for this species in la March. The first brood generally mo conspicuous than th second, though or because the trees hav less leaf, and there a fewer other butterfli aroun

Large Blue

Maculinea arion

Extinct as a native butterfly in 1979, the Large Blue has since been successfully re-introduced to a number of sites where careful management of the habitat has ensured its survival.

Re-established Residen

Wingspan: male 38–48 m
female 42–52 m
Chrysalis: 13 m
Caterpillar: 15 m
Egg: 0·5 (w) × 0·3 mm (

IDENTIFICATION

ADULT : Its name is misleading, for though it is the largest of our blue butterflies, its size is variable, and many individuals are smaller than the Chalkhill Blue. Both sexes have black-edged, blue wings, with distinctive black spotting on the forewings, although the larger female is generally more heavily marked than the male. The black spots on the upperside are unique among British blues, and are the diagnostic field mark.

CHRYSALIS : Sepia-brown, and formed within the nests of ants.

CATERPILLAR : Pale, stout-bodied, and resembling an ant grub.

EGG : White, and laid on the flowers of Wild Thyme.

BEHAVIOUR

Adult males tend to be most active on sunny mornings, patrolling back and forth across their breeding grounds. On hot afternoons they roost in the shade, usually emerging later to take nectar from Wild Thyme. The life span is about five days.

The most extraordinary feature of the Large Blue's life cycle is its dependence on one species of red ant, *Myrmica sabuleti*. The ants take the Large Blue caterpillars into their nests, where the caterpillars feast on ant grubs. Surviving caterpillars hibernate in the nest, and pupate the following May.

HABITAT

This species requires well-drained, unimproved grassland, closely cropped by rabbits, sheep, cattle or ponies. Acidic coastal grassland is preferred, but it used to occur on calcareous clay soils. The presence of abundant colonies of the red ant *Myrmica sabuleti* is, of course, vital.

POPULATION AND CONSERVATION

Re-introduction of Swedish butterflies to specially prepared sites in southern England started in 1983. The work is now co-ordinated by Butterfly Conservation in partnership with a number of conservation bodies. As a result, the Large Blue is now firmly re-established at several sites. However, the sites depend on continuing management and drought is a potential problem.

WHERE TO FIN

The sites where the Larg Blue has bee re-introduced have bee kept secret for th butterfly's securit However, open days certain West Countr colonies are no arranged every summe and a public site planne

OBSERVATION TIP

Sunny mornings in ear July are best for viewin this delightful butterfl

Duke of Burgundy

Hamearis lucina

Localised Resident

Wingspan:	29–34 m
Chrysalis:	9 m
Caterpillar:	16 m
Egg:	0·6 (w) × 0·6 mm

This species has suffered a widespread decline in recent decades, and its scattered colonies are now highly localised.

IDENTIFICATION

ADULT : A spring-flying butterfly with a fritillary-like appearance. It can be readily separated from the fritillaries by shape and behaviour. Alternatively, look for the two bands of white spots that run parallel on the underwing, and the white spots along the edge of both the forewing and hindwing. Confusion with the Chequered Skipper (*page 30*) is also possible, but note that the ranges of the two do not overlap in Britain.

CHRYSALIS : Hairy and spotted, and formed on or close to the ground.

CATERPILLAR : Dark brown, and short and hairy.

EGG : Spherical, laid in small groups on the leaves of either Primrose or Cowslip.

BEHAVIOUR

Lives in small, compact colonies. Territorial males are most conspicuous as they defend their chosen bush or grass tussock from rivals, with the resulting fight leading to spectacular aerial encounters. This is one of the most pugnacious of butterflies. Resting males sit with their wings half open. Females are much more elusive, spending most of the time resting, or flying low looking for egg-laying sites.

HABITAT

Two types are favoured: chalk or limestone grassland, or clearings in areas of ancient woodland. It likes its foodplants to be growing amongst tussocky vegetation, and on downland it is usually found on north-facing or west-facing slopes.

POPULATION AND CONSERVATION

There has been an alarming decline in the number of colonies in recent decades, due to the intensification of agriculture on its favoured downland sites, and the cessation of coppicing in old woodlands. The resurgence of rabbits has also created a problem, as they crop the sward too tightly, and destroy suitable foodplants.

WHERE TO FIN[D]

Limestone grassland in th[e] Cotswolds, and the cha[lk] downs of Wiltshir[e,] Hampshire and Susse[x.] Managed nature reserve[s] such as Martin Dow[n] NNR in Hampshire, offe[r] the best chance [of] succes[s.]

OBSERVATION TIP[S]

This is a spring butterfl[y] and most numerous i[n] late May. Best looked fo[r] on warm, sunny day[s.]

White Admiral

Limenitis camilla

Localised Resident

Wingspan: male 54–64 n
female 58–66 n
Chrysalis: 22 n
Caterpillar: 25–29 n
Egg: 0·9 (w) × 0·9 mm

An elegant and attractive butterfly that is on the increase. It has a huge range in Europe and Asia, and can be found as far east as Japan.

IDENTIFICATION

ADULT : Although easy to identify when close, from a distance the White Admiral could be mistaken for the Purple Emperor (*page 98*). Although the uppersides are similar, the underside of the White Admiral lacks the 'eye' of the larger Purple Emperor. The smaller White Admiral's wings are more rounded and it has a daintier, gliding flight. The sexes are almost identical.

CHRYSALIS : Unusually shaped, and coloured green and brown, resembling a dead Honeysuckle leaf.

CATERPILLAR : Spiny, brown at first Ca , turning bright green after the final moult, with a whitish line along the spiracles CaF .

EGG : Spherical, laid singly on Honeysuckle, the sole foodplant.

BEHAVIOUR

Unrivalled among British butterflies for its graceful and agile flight. White Admirals propel themselves with a quick whirr of the wings, followed by long glides. Though the adults spend a lot of time in the tree canopy, they will also come down to ground level, where they are particularly attracted by Bramble blossom.

HABITAT

This butterfly typically favours sunny rides in broad-leaved woodland in the southern half of England. However, it can also be found in young coniferous plantations, before the growing trees shade out the ground cover. Its most important requirement is a plentiful supply of Honeysuckle, the caterpillar's foodplant, though White Admirals are often absent from woods where conditions appear ideal.

POPULATION AND CONSERVATION

This is a species that has increased and spread during the last 50 years, and is more widespread in Britain today than it has ever been in the past. Its range now extends northwards to Suffolk, Norfolk, Lincolnshire and the West Midlands. It is unusual to see more than two or three butterflies at a time, as population densities are usually low. A potentially serious threat to its future may come from the spread of Muntjac deer, for this alien species browses on Honeysuckle.

WHERE TO FIN

Though most easily foun
in deciduous woodlands
southern Englan
(especially Hampshir
Dorset, Sussex ar
Surrey), it can now b
seen in many woodlan
in East Anglia and th
West and East Midland

OBSERVATION TIP

Best looked for in sunn
rides or glades
deciduous woodlan
with a dominance of oa
and hazel. Most frequent
seen well when feedin
on patches of Brambl

Purple Emperor

Apatura iris

After a decline, there are signs of a range re-expansion in south-eastern England, but still scarce and localised.

IDENTIFICATION

ADULT : With a good view, there is no mistaking a male Purple Emperor, due to a combination of its large size, distinctive white-on-black markings, and glorious purple sheen, although this can only be seen at certain angles as it depends on the refraction of light. The female is slightly larger, has bolder markings, and lacks the purple sheen. Colour variations are rare.

CHRYSALIS : Pale green and closely resembling a sallow leaf.

CATERPILLAR : Very well camouflaged: green when first hatched **Ca**, but by November has turned brown ready for winter hibernation. Post-hibernation spring caterpillars are green, with distinctive 'horns' on the head **CaF**.

EGG : Dome-shaped, green, laid singly on the foodplant, usually Goat Willow but sometimes Common Willow.

BEHAVIOUR

The many detailed studies of the behaviour of the Purple Emperor have found that males of this species are most easily observed in the morning, usually between 10 and 11 am, when they will descend to the ground to sip from puddles. It has also been noted that males can be attracted to rotting flesh, or even animal droppings. Male Purple Emperors will remain around a so-called 'master tree' – a particularly favoured tree in the forest and usually an oak. The male will perch here, wings half open, waiting to intercept a passing female, or chase off a rival male. These 'master trees' may be used for year after year.

HABITAT

This is a woodland butterfly, and is seldom found far from mature deciduous or mixed forest. The only essential requirement for a population of Emperors is a plentiful supply of its foodplants. Purple Emperors are powerful fliers and, rarely, wandering individuals may be encountered following hedgerows, or even crossing open fields.

POPULATION AND CONSERVATION

For much of the 20th century this species declined throughout its range in southern England, but in recent years there has been a welcome resurgence, and a modest re-expansion. It has been found in a number of counties from which it had long been regarded as absent, including Kent, Northamptonshire and east Devon. Its survival depends on the sensitive management of ancient woodland, and the retention of willows.

Wingspan: male 70–78 r
female 76–92 ■
Chrysalis: 30–35 ■
Caterpillar: 35–40 r
Egg: 1·0 mm

WHERE TO FIN

Relatively common in t
right habitat in the Surr
and Sussex Weald, and
larger woods in cent
southern Englan

OBSERVATION TI

Look for on sunny days
late July around m
morning . Bait (such
rotting banana) can
used, or, if dry, ma
shallow puddles ir
woodland ride. Look f
patrolling males high in t
canopy, and try to find
'master tre

Butterflies shown at 1·2x

Red Admiral
Vanessa atalanta

This is a familiar and widespread species throughout Britain, though numbers each year depend on migration from the continent.

Abundant Migrant		
Wingspan:	male	64–72
	female	70–78
Chrysalis:		22–24
Caterpillar:		35
Egg:		0·8 mm

IDENTIFICATION

ADULT : Unmistakable, for no other British butterfly has the same distinctive combination of black, white and red. The sexes are similar although males are slightly smaller.

CHRYSALIS : Invariably to be found at the top of a nettle, within a feeding shelter made by the caterpillar. This is the easiest chrysalis to find of any British butterfly.

CATERPILLAR : The solitary caterpillar occurs in several colour forms, ranging from black to yellow.

EGG : The eggs are laid singly on the upper surfaces of Common Nettle leaves.

BEHAVIOUR

A strongly migratory species: the British population depends almost entirely on immigration each year from the continent, for very few adults manage to hibernate successfully here. The first major influxes are in late May and early June. The females arrive already mated, and it is their offspring that we see in the summer and autumn. This species is usually at its most abundant in September, when fallen fruit will often attract considerable numbers. In mild, sunny autumns, it is not unusual to see Red Admirals on the wing well into November. Many undertake a southerly migration back towards the continent at this time.

HABITAT

An adaptable species that can occur in almost any flower-rich habitat throughout Britain. Gardens with flowering buddleias are particularly popular. It requires vigorous young Common Nettles for breeding.

POPULATION AND CONSERVATION

In most years this is one of our commonest and most widespread butterflies. Numbers have even increased in recent years. Thanks to the abundance of its foodplants, the future of this magnificent butterfly seems assured.

WHERE TO FIN
Almost anywhe

OBSERVATION TI
An easy butterfly to wat
as it feeds on nectar
autumn, Red Admirals c
become 'drunk' wh
feeding on ferment
fruit, making them fing
tan

F

Ca

Ad

Painted Lady

Vanessa cardui

A handsome migrant butterfly that in some years is common throughout much of Britain and Ireland, but in others is scarce or even absent.

Regular Migrant

Wingspan: male 58–70 r
female 62–74 r
Chrysalis: 25 r
Caterpillar: 30 r
Egg: 0·65 mm

IDENTIFICATION

ADULT : An easy butterfly to identify, thanks to a combination of its powerful flight and distinctive colouring. However, it should be noted that adults vary significantly in size and that the beautiful salmon-pink of a freshly emerged Painted Lady fades to orange-brown during its long life. Badly faded and tatty individuals are not uncommon.

CHRYSALIS : Suspended under vegetation, and occurs in two colour forms.

CATERPILLAR : The solitary, spiny, black-bodied, white-dotted caterpillar spins a succession of silk tents, before finally emerging to feed openly after its last moult.

EGG : Small, oval, green and relatively easy to find on the foodplants, particularly thistles.

BEHAVIOUR

A highly migratory species, with the first butterflies of the year to reach us probably direct migrants from North Africa. With its fast and powerful flight, this species can travel considerable distances with relative ease. Once settled, males establish themselves in a territory, vigorously investigating any object that attracts its attention. Both the male and female feed frequently on flowers, and in years of abundance it is not uncommon to see many individuals feeding together.

HABITAT

This wide-ranging migrant can occur anywhere, but it favours dry, open areas and avoids woodlands.

POPULATION AND CONSERVATION

Britain's population depends wholly on migration. In an exceptional year, millions of Painted Ladies can be found in Britain, even extending as far north as Orkney and Shetland. Though an adult has been recorded over-wintering in Cornwall, it is thought that the entire British population effectively dies out each winter, and re-colonisation depends on immigration the following spring.

WHERE TO FIN

Due to its stro
migratory instincts, can b
found virtually anywher

OBSERVATION TIP

Easy to approach close
when feeding or basking
the sunshine. In yea
when few adults mana
to reach our shores, it c
be totally absent fro
many counties, though
can generally be four
along the south coa

Small Tortoiseshell
Aglais urticae

Widely distributed throughout Britain and Ireland, and can be found in almost every month.

Abundant Resident

Wingspan: male 45–55 m
female 52–62 m
Chrysalis: 20–22 m
Caterpillar: 32 m
Egg: 0·75 (w) × 0·85 mm

IDENTIFICATION
ADULT : Readily identified by its striking and attractive pattern, shared by both sexes. Look for the delightful blue edges to both wings. Cool temperatures produce darker individuals, while high temperatures can produce the aberration *semi-ichnusoides* si . A hot British summer produces the brightest individuals. The Small Tortoiseshell can only really be confused with the exceedingly rare migrant Large Tortoiseshell (*page 154*), which is larger, duller, and lacks the white spots on the forewing.

CHRYSALIS : Variable in colour from golden to brown.

CATERPILLAR : Black body, finely dotted with white, and with broken bands of yellow on either side. These are warning colours, for the body contains poisons. The caterpillars are found in groups in white silken webs which are easy to spot in patches of Common Nettle.

EGG : The pale green egg is laid in large clusters on the underside of Common Nettle leaves.

BEHAVIOUR
Individuals that have hibernated usually emerge for the first time on warm, sunny days in March or April, though earlier sightings are common in southern England.

Studies of adults have shown that the males tend to be more mobile in the morning, when they feed and bask in the sun. In the afternoon they set up temporary territories, which they defend from rivals, and court passing females.

In contrast, individuals that are going to hibernate show no interest in courtship, but spend their days feeding up in preparation for hibernation, which they will enter as early as late July or August.

HABITAT
Cosmopolitan, and can be found almost anywhere, from the tops of mountains to city centres.

POPULATION AND CONSERVATION
Though this butterfly seems always to have been widespread, numbers do fluctuate markedly from year to year. Southern populations have at least two and sometimes three broods a year. This is one of the most successful butterflies in Britain, and its future looks secure.

WHERE TO FIN
Look first in your ow
garden, where flowerir
buddleias are a
irresistible drav

OBSERVATION TIP
One of the easie
butterflies to find ar
watch. Look out for (bu
don't disturb) hibernatir
individuals in garden shed
attics, or church tower

Peacock
Inachis io

A handsome and familiar butterfly that is continuing to expand its range northwards in Britain.

Abundant Resident

Wingspan: male 63–68 m
female 67–75 m
Chrysalis: 25–29 m
Caterpillar: 42 m
Egg: 0·8 mm (

IDENTIFICATION
ADULT : Unmistakable thanks to the large 'eyes' in the corner of both front and hindwings. The beautifully camouflaged underside is almost black.

CHRYSALIS : Variable in colour, difficult to found in the wild.

CATERPILLAR : Black, white-speckled, with long spines and found in groups within a silken web until fully grown, when they may be found singly.

EGG : Laid in large batches on the underside of Common Nettle leaves.

BEHAVIOUR
Adults that have hibernated are one of the first butterflies on the wing on warm spring days. They feed during the morning, then the males establish territories, from which they see off intruding males or pursue females. For summer adults, the chief preoccupation is feeding in preparation for hibernation, which they usually enter in early September. Dark, sheltered crevices in trees, garden sheds or even church towers are popular for hibernation.

HABITAT
Almost anywhere, for this is a highly adaptable species. The best sites are where favoured nectar plants are plentiful (willows in spring, and teasels, thistles and buddleias in summer). Large nettle patches are required for egg laying.

POPULATION AND CONSERVATION
Widespread, and continuing to extend its range northwards. A species that is thriving in Britain.

WHERE TO FIN
Almost anywhere, b
sheltered woodlar
clearings and gardens a
favoure

OBSERVATION TIP
Watch how this butter
flashes its wings
potential enemies, using
flashing 'eyes' to war
them o

Ad

F

Ca

Ch

Comma

Polygonia c-album

Common Resident

Wingspan: male 50–64 m

Chrysalis: 21 m

Caterpillar: 32–35 m

Egg: 0·65 mm (w) × 0·8 (

A century ago, this handsome butterfly was a rarity in Britain. Since then it has enjoyed a reversal in its fortunes, and today is a common butterfly throughout almost all of England and Wales, though it is only a vagrant to Scotland and Ireland.

IDENTIFICATION

ADULT : With its wings closed, this is a well-camouflaged butterfly, resembling a dead, ragged leaf, though look for the distinctive white comma mark on the underwing that gives this butterfly its name. The adults come in two colour forms: early spring caterpillars produce the form *hutchinsoni* **h** , which have golden brown undersides. The 'normal' Comma is a rich tawny-red. Its gliding flight and colouration can suggest a fritillary, but the scalloped wing shape is unmistakable.

CHRYSALIS : Resembles the underwing of the adult, for it has a beautiful dead-leaf camouflage.

CATERPILLAR : Black, banded with orange-brown. At first feeds on the under-surface of a leaf; when larger feeds exclusively on the upper surface, where a distinctive white splash on the back helps to protect it by making it resemble a bird dropping.

EGG : Laid singly on the upperside of a leaf of its foodplant: Common Nettle, Hop and elms.

BEHAVIOUR

One of the first butterflies to be seen on the wing, with adults often emerging for their first spring flights in late February or early March. The males feed early in the morning and again in the late afternoon, but much of the day is spent patrolling in search of a mate. The flight is fast and easy, with a rapid whirr of wings, followed by long glides. In summer, Commas are frequent visitors to flowering buddleias, while in the autumn they are also attracted to fallen fruit.

HABITAT

This species likes open woodland and woodland edges, but is often found in gardens, where they range in search of nectar and rotting fruit.

POPULATION AND CONSERVATION

The fall and rise of the Comma still intrigues entomologists, for no-one has managed to explain it conclusively. It continues to thrive in England and Wales, is still expanding its range northwards, and is poised to recolonise Scotland. It may even colonise Ireland, where a few have been seen in recent years.

WHERE TO FIN

Anywhere in suitab habitat in the souther half of Britain, but watc out for wanderir individuals as far north a the Lake District an possibly even Scotland

OBSERVATION TIP

In spring, look fo Commas feeding o willow catkins. Thoug never numerous, this is widespread and commo butterfly, and one that relatively easy to find i almost any month fror March to Octobe

Small Pearl-bordered Fritillary
Boloria selene

Once a common butterfly throughout most of Britain, but now lost from much of its former range in the east. It remains widespread in Scotland and Wales.

Declining Resident

Wingspan: male 35–41 m
female 38–44 m
Chrysalis: 15 m
Caterpillar: 21 m
Egg: 0·65 mm (

IDENTIFICATION

ADULT : This species is easily confused with the very similar Pearl-bordered Fritillary (*page 112*). The flight periods overlap, though Small Pearl-bordered Fritillary emerges later, and can still be seen in early July. Both species have an occasional second brood in August. The markings of the upperside of the wings of the two species are very similar, and both show lots of variation. However, note the much more contrasting underside of this species, which is a reliable field mark. The seven pearls along the outer edge of the hindwing (from which it takes its name) are framed with black chevrons, whilst those of the Pearl-bordered Fritillary are framed with red.

CHRYSALIS : Dark brown with silvery points.

CATERPILLAR : Dark brown, with yellow spines and black bristles.

EGG : Pale yellow, conical and strongly ribbed; laid on or near violets, usually Common Dog-violet or Marsh Violet.

BEHAVIOUR

Males patrol with the attractive, gliding flight typical of the small fritillaries, keeping low and often pausing to sunbathe with wings spread wide. Egg-laying females flutter close to the ground, frequently alighting as they search for violets on which to lay their eggs.

WHERE TO FIN
Most easily found
Scotland and Wales.
southern England, it is ver
localise

HABITAT

Several distinct habitats are used in Britain. In the south it is usually found in woodland glades and clearings, whilst in the north and west damp grassland and moorland are favoured. Scottish colonies are usually found in sheep-grazed or deer-grazed open wood-pasture, usually with patches of Bracken and scrub. It also occurs in dune slacks and coastal cliffs.

OBSERVATION TIP
In northern and wester
Britain, this butterf
occurs in low densitie
over extensive areas, but
best looked for in dam
sheltered areas where th
foodplant, Marsh Viole
grows. Peak abundance
in mid-June, though usual
later in Scotlan

POPULATION AND CONSERVATION

Though widespread and locally abundant in Scotland, Wales and the West Country, numbers have declined dramatically elsewhere in southern England. The decline is thought to be due to the cessation of coppicing. In other parts of its range, the greatest threats are the loss of unfertilised damp grassland, and the degradation of moorland due to forestry or overgrazing.

Pearl-bordered Fritillary

Boloria euphrosyne

The earliest of the British fritillaries to appear on the wing, usually emerging in the second week of May.

Threatened Resident

Wingspan: male 38–46 m
female 43–47 m
Chrysalis: 14 m
Caterpillar: 20–25 m
Eg: 0·8 mm (

IDENTIFICATION

ADULT : All the small fritillaries are easily confused. This species can be separated from all others, except the Small Pearl-bordered, by the seven silver pearls that edge the underside of the hindwing. It is the underwing that is the key to telling the two pearl-bordered species apart: on the Pearl-bordered it is more uniformly golden and lacking in contrast, although there are two bright silver patches on the inner hindwing that the Small Pearl-bordered lacks. Look, also, for the black central spot on the hindwing; this is smaller in the Pearl-bordered Fritillary.

CHRYSALIS : Looks like a dead leaf – grey-brown with silver spots.

CATERPILLAR : Black, with a row of white spots on either side and black or yellow spines.

EGG : White or pale yellow, and strongly ribbed, laid on or near violets, mainly Common Dog-violet.

BEHAVIOUR

While females are generally inconspicuous, on warm days the males spend much of their time patrolling their territory, moving apparently effortlessly with glides and small, quick flaps of their wings. Both sexes are attracted to yellow and purple plants for nectaring, with Bugle particularly popular.

HABITAT

Three habitats are favoured. In southern England, it likes recently coppiced woodland clearings. In the West Country, it is usually to be found where there is a mixture of well-drained grassland, dense Bracken and light scrub. Scottish populations prefer south-facing woodland edges, along with dense Bracken, and grazing by sheep and deer.

POPULATION AND CONSERVATION

One of our most rapidly declining butterflies. The virtual cessation of coppicing has been its downfall in southern and eastern England, but it often responds well when efforts are made to manage woodland for it. In the West Country, it depends on traditional low-intensity grazing, while in Scotland, efforts to increase the area of native woodland and the exclusion of sheep and deer are likely to hasten its disappearance.

WHERE TO FIN

A number of woodlar nature reserves in Susse Hampshire and Dors are managed specially fc this species. In the We Country, the Dartmoc area remains a strongho

OBSERVATION TIP

In an exceptionally ear spring, it may emerge early April, but in norther Scotland the ma emergence will be sever weeks later. In a good yea look out for a secon brood in the south Augus

High Brown Fritillary

Argynnis adippe

Endangered Residen[t]

Wingspan:	male	55–69
	female	62–75
Chrysalis:		20
Caterpillar:		38
Egg:		0·8 mm

One of our most endangered and rapidly declining butterflies, restricted almost entirely to western Britain, from the Lake District south to Dartmoor. Less than 50 colonies remain.

IDENTIFICATION

ADULT : This large, bright fritillary can be confused with the Dark Green Fritillary (*page 116*). Separating the two is difficult unless you see the underside. The High Brown takes its name from the brownish crescents around the outer silver patches, although the best field mark is the red-ringed spots on the hindwing, a feature the Dark Green lacks. The High Brown's forewing is less rounded and more angular than that of the Dark Green. Females are slightly larger than males, and are more heavily marked with black.

CHRYSALIS : Variegated dark to mid-brown, resembling a dead leaf.

CATERPILLAR : Either dark, reddish-brown, or, more often, a pale, greenish-brown. There is a distinctive white line down the back, running through a series of triangular black markings. The caterpillars look like dead Bracken fronds and are found feeding on violet, usually Common Dog-violet, and basking in the sun.

EGG : Cone-shaped, pink when first laid on twigs, dead leaves or stones near the ground, turning slate-grey with age.

BEHAVIOUR

Only really active in hot sunshine. Male High Brown Fritillaries have a fast, powerful flight, from which they divert to investigate anything resembling a female. Males are not unduly aggressive or territorial. They are best approached while feeding, when often oblivious. Both sexes frequently soar among tree tops, roosting there at night and remaining there all day if the weather is poor.

HABITAT

Once regarded as chiefly a woodland butterfly, this species is now associated with areas of open scrub and rough grassland in western Britain. (The eastern, woodland-dwelling populations almost all died out between 1950 and 1980.) Bracken-covered south-facing slopes are a favoured habitat, although these colonies are now very small.

POPULATION AND CONSERVATION

Following its rapid decline in the second half of the 20th century, this butterfly is being assisted by careful habitat management. Most of the Lake District colonies are within nature reserves where some are thriving.

WHERE TO FIN[D]

There are colonies Dartmoor, Exmoor a the Malvern Hills but 1 easiest place to see t species is on the southe hills of the Lake Distr[ict]

OBSERVATION TIP[S]

This species is particula[rly] active on hot, summ[er] days, when the ma[les] never seem to stop flyi[ng] Dark Green Fritillar[ies] may occur on the sa[me] site, but it is unusual the two to be commo[n] the same area. Both se[xes] like to feed on Bramb[le]

114

Dark Green Fritillary
Argynnis aglaja

A widely distributed, fast-flying butterfly typical of downland and coastal dunes.

Widespread Resident	
Wingspan:	58–68 m
Chrysalis:	19 m
Caterpillar:	35–40 m
Egg:	1·0 mm

IDENTIFICATION

ADULT : Very similar in size, shape and appearance to the High Brown Fritillary (*page 114*), and most readily separated by its much wider range. The Dark Green Fritillary favours open country and is a larger, more powerful butterfly than all our other fritillaries except the woodland-preferring Silver-washed Fritillary (*page 118*). The Dark Green gets its name from the distinctive green wash on the underwings, a feature common to both sexes. The golden ground colour of the wings tends to be paler in females, especially towards the edges. Scottish butterflies tend to be more heavily marked than those from the south.

CHRYSALIS : Reddish-brown with black markings, and a distinctly curved abdomen.

CATERPILLAR : Velvety black, with black stripes and a row of orange-red spots along the flanks.

EGG : Cone-shaped and creamy yellow, laid singly on or close to violets, soon becoming dull maroon.

BEHAVIOUR

An elegant, fast-flying butterfly. On warm, sunny days the males patrol their territory incessantly, their distinctive flight involving a number of rapid wing beats followed by a smooth, fast glide. The females tend to remain hidden until they are ready to lay their eggs, when they can be identified by a more fluttering flight as they search for violets. Whilst hidden, the females are located by the males by scent.

HABITAT

This is a butterfly of flower-rich unimproved grasslands, though it occasionally occurs in woodland rides and clearings. Their choice of habitat is surprisingly catholic, for they can be found on chalk and limestone downland, on acid grassland, moorland and (in Scotland particularly) on coastal dunes.

POPULATION AND CONSERVATION

Though the most widespread and common fritillary in Britain, this spectacular butterfly has been lost from many parts of its former range since 1960 due to changing patterns of land use. However, its adaptability, and its tolerance of wetter and cooler conditions than other fritillaries, has helped its survival. Loss of the flower-rich grasslands it favours, and the subsequent fragmentation of populations are its greatest threats.

WHERE TO FIN

Sufficiently widespread be relatively easy to find suitable habitat, especi Scottish coastal dunes, t North and South Dow and Exmoor a Dartmo

OBSERVATION TI

Only really active sunny days, when usu seen flying. The best tir to see a male perched early or late in the c when purple flowe attract the

F

M

M

F

Ca

Ch

Silver-washed Fritillary
Argynnis paphia

This handsome butterfly is the largest of the British fritillaries. Its population is increasing once again after a long period of decline in the 20th century.

IDENTIFICATION

ADULT : The easiest of our fritillaries to identify, due to its large size, distinctive flight and preferred habitat. The rich golden-brown wings with clear black markings are typical of a fritillary, but the subtle silver washes on the underwing of both sexes separate it from other species. Males can be easily told from females by the four black ridges on the veins of each forewing. Females also have more extensive, heavier black markings, and look rather darker than the male. A distinctive form called *valezina* (*see page 148*) occurs in some populations, particularly in central-southern England, where up to 15% of the females have a greenish-grey ground-colour to their wings and the underwings appear distinctly pink. When seen in flight, a *valezina* looks like a different species altogether.

CHRYSALIS : As with other fritillaries, camouflaged to resemble a dead leaf and extremely difficult to find.

CATERPILLAR : Hard to find, but easily recognised by the characteristic yellow lines; feeds exclusively on violets, especially Common Dog-violet.

EGG : Laid singly in the crevices of the bark of tree trunks.

BEHAVIOUR

A powerful butterfly with a fast, gliding flight. Adults often fly high around the tops of trees, but they will readily drop down in search of nectar (Bramble is particularly popular), or to chase a potential mate. When feeding they can be approached readily. Though most active when the sun is shining, they will still fly on lightly overcast days. Females will venture into shadier parts of the woodland to lay their eggs.

HABITAT

This is a butterfly of broad-leaved woodland, particularly favouring sunny rides and glades in oak woodlands. However, in Somerset, Devon, Cornwall and southern Ireland, it is not unusual to find this species wandering along well-wooded hedgerows and sheltered, sunken lanes.

POPULATION AND CONSERVATION

In Victorian times the Silver-washed Fritillary was much more common than it is today, its range even extending as far north as Scotland. Its range contracted markedly between then and the 1970s, and while its range has expanded since, the population has not increased significantly.

118

Localised Resident

Wingspan: male 69–76 r
female 73–80 r
Chrysalis: 22 n
Caterpillar: 38 n
Egg: 1·0 mm

WHERE TO FIN

It is worth checking a large oak woodland southern or wester England. The New Fore is a good area, but th species is not as abundan there as it once wa

OBSERVATION TIP

If present in a woodlan this species is genera easy to observe. Thoug invariably found in discret colonies, in hot summe individuals may wander f from known colonie Numbers are highest late July/early Augus

Marsh Fritillary

Euphydryas aurinia

The Marsh Fritillary is a scarce and localised colonial species that declined severely during the 20th century.

Threatened Resident

Wingspan: male 30–42 r
female 40–50 r
Chrysalis: 12–15 r
Caterpillar: 26–30 r
Egg: 0·8 mm

IDENTIFICATION

ADULT : This beautiful butterfly is highly variable in its markings and colouration, and different colonies can have their own characteristics. Females tend to be larger and paler than the males. However, it is relatively easy to identify and the only likely confusion is with the Heath Fritillary (*page 124*). The most obvious difference between the two is the bright, checkerboard look of the Marsh Fritillary's upperwings. In contrast, the Heath Fritillary is darker and more uniform in its markings, the underwing has brighter and more contrasting markings, and a white band on the hindwing. The front edge of the wing of the Marsh Fritillary is slightly concave, while that of the Heath Fritillary is convex.

CHRYSALIS : Greyish-white with yellow and black spots.

CATERPILLAR : Black, with reddish-brown legs. Gregarious at first, living in a silken web, becoming solitary when fully grown.

EGG : Laid in large batches on the undersides of Devil's-bit Scabious leaves. Pale yellow when fresh, darkening with age.

BEHAVIOUR

Rather slow-flying in comparison with other fritillaries, keeping low to the ground. Most adults seldom fly more than 100 m from where they emerged. Females mate within a few hours of emerging, and are so full of eggs that they crawl in the vegetation and can only fly short distances. Once their eggs have been laid, they will fly longer distances from flower to flower.

HABITAT

The name Marsh Fritillary is misleading, for though this butterfly favours damp, tussocky grassland where its foodplant grows, it is not really a marshland species. In a population explosion, colonies can be found in woodland clearings or other grasslands. During the last century, this species colonised chalk and limestone downland in the Cotswolds, Dorset and Wiltshire, where it can still be found, as well as in damp grasslands in western counties.

POPULATION AND CONSERVATION

Drainage of damp meadows has been the downfall of this species. Conserving this fast-declining species is a major challenge. This is because of its specific requirement of abundant Devil's-bit Scabious in an extensive area of habitat subject to low intensity grazing. Marsh Fritillary colonies are subject to huge fluctuations in size; a thriving colony with thousands of adults in one year, may be extinct a few years later. Parasitic wasps are known to play a major role in such events.

WHERE TO FIN

The best places to se
this butterfly are the Cu
grasslands of north Dev
and Cornwall, the milita
ranges of Salisbury Pla
the heathy commons
west Wales, weste
Ireland and Isl

OBSERVATION TIP

Best seen at know
colonies on sunny days
mid-June, though the flig
period extends from mi
May through to early Ju
Easy to photograph,
they can be approache
easily when feedir

Glanville Fritillary
Melitaea cinxia

This attractive butterfly is on the northernmost edge of its range in Britain, so has always been our rarest fritillary.

Rare Resident

Wingspan:	male 38–46 m
	female 44–52 m
Chrysalis:	13–15 m
Caterpillar:	25 m
Egg:	0·9 mm (

IDENTIFICATION

ADULT : The Glanville Fritillary's specialised habitat and restricted range makes identification in the UK easy: it is confined to a few sites on undercliffs of the Isle of Wight and south Hampshire, where no other fritillaries are likely to be found. The butterfly can be identified by the delicate markings of the underside of the hindwing, which has a row of submarginal spots, a feature shared only with the Marsh Fritillary (*page 120*).

CHRYSALIS : Greyish-purple, with black spots.

CATERPILLAR : Black, bristly and gregarious, living in silken webs.

EGG : Yellow, and thimble-shaped, they are laid in large batches on the underside of leaves of Ribwort Plantain.

BEHAVIOUR

Male Glanville Fritillaries are among the most active and agile of butterflies. Their flight is swift, with glides interspersed by rapid wing-beats. Though the females tend to be less conspicuous, remaining hidden for long periods, they also fly with agility.

HABITAT

On the Isle of Wight this butterfly can be found in three distinct habitats. It is usually associated with sheltered undercliffs, where land slips have produced deep valleys, or chines, with a profusion of wildflowers, including its favoured nectar plants, Common Bird's-foot-trefoil and Thrift. It can also be found on the tops of cliffs, and on south-facing downland. Undercliff colonies tend to be the largest and more permanent.

POPULATION AND CONSERVATION

Though vulnerable due to its restricted range, its status has changed little in recent decades. However, since the early 1990s a small colony has been established on the coast of Hampshire. There have been many attempts to introduce this butterfly elsewhere, although all have been unsuccessful except for a small colony in Somerset. This species is largely dependent on a specialised transitory and unstable habitat. Its future depends on the continued creation, by natural means or otherwise, of fresh habitat.

WHERE TO FIND
The south coast of the Isl of Wight, but much mor widespread and commo on the near Continer

OBSERVATION TIP
As it is so active, this is a easy butterfly to see in th right habitat. Pea numbers occur in earl June, but soon start t declin

Heath Fritillary

Melitaea athalia

Though one of our rarest and most localised species, this sedentary butterfly has been saved from the brink of extinction in England.

Endangered Resident

Wingspan:	male 39–44 m
	female 42–47 m
Chrysalis:	12·5 m
Caterpillar:	22–25 m
Egg:	0·5 mm (

IDENTIFICATION

ADULT : This is one of the smallest of our fritillaries, and can be readily recognised by its generally dark colouring – although the larger female is usually slightly paler than the male. The species with which it is most likely to be confused in Britain are the larger and brighter Marsh Fritillary (*page 120*) and the two species of pearl-bordered fritillary (*pages 110,112*), both of which show seven silver pearls along the borders of each hindwing. The Heath Fritillary's restricted range and its sedentary nature rules out any natural occurrence away from the few known colonies.

CHRYSALIS : White, mottled with brown and black, and usually found in a dead leaf close to the ground.

CATERPILLAR: Black, with greyish-white spots and yellow-orange spines.

EGG : Pale-yellow, ribbed and thimble-shaped, invariably laid in large batches on the undersides of leaves.

BEHAVIOUR

Few British butterflies are more dependent on the sun than this species. On warm, sunny days, the males spend much of their time on the wing, flying with short flicks and flat-winged glides low to the ground. In contrast, the inconspicuous females spend most of their short lives (5-10 days) basking, or hidden in vegetation.

HABITAT

Three different types of habitat are favoured. In Kent and Essex the colonies are in coppiced woodland on acid soils where Common Cow-wheat, the preferred foodplant, is abundant. On Exmoor, it favours sheltered combes (valleys) where the caterpillars will also eat Foxglove. In Devon and Cornwall the colonies are in abandoned hay meadows, where Ribwort Plantain and Germander Speedwell are the favoured foodplants.

POPULATION AND CONSERVATION

Detailed studies have revealed the precise habitat requirements of this specialised, warmth-loving species. It was the cessation of coppicing that originally led to its downfall. The colonies in Essex and Kent now depend upon conservation management involving a coppicing regime. This rare and localised butterfly's future in Britain depends upon continuing, careful habitat management.

WHERE TO FIN

The best place to look fe this butterfly is in Blea Woods, near Canterbur Kent. On Exmoor: searc for it on the south-facin slopes of sheltered combe

OBSERVATION TIP

Sunny, warm days a essential to see th species on the wing. seldom flies if th temperature is belo 18°C. The Exmoo colonies emerge in mic June, a fortnight earlie than those in Kent ar Esse

124

Speckled Wood
Pararge aegeria

Common Resident

Wingspan: male 46–52 m
female 48–56 m
Chrysalis: 18 m
Caterpillar: 28 m
Egg: 0·8 mm (

After range contractions during the late 19th and early 20th century, this species has been steadily regaining ground, and is still recolonising areas in eastern and northern England and Scotland.

IDENTIFICATION

ADULT : The cream-on-chocolate wings of the Speckled Wood make this an easy butterfly to identify. Females have larger yellow patches than the males, while the later broods of both sexes tend to be darker than those that emerge earlier in the year. The Scottish form *oblita* **Mo** is darker with pale cream patches.

CHRYSALIS : A delicate shade of green.

CATERPILLAR : Yellowish-green, with a white-bordered dark green stripe along the middle of the back and lines along side.

EGG : Almost spherical, pale, and laid singly on blades of a variety of grasses; Cock's-foot, Yorkshire-fog and False Brome being favourites. In spring and early autumn, eggs are laid on plants in open, sunlit situations; in summer they are laid on plants in shaded woodland.

BEHAVIOUR

The Speckled Wood's habit of drinking honeydew high in the tree canopy goes largely unobserved, but in spring and late summer (when honeydew is in short supply), individuals will take nectar from flowers. Males spend their days either basking in patches of sunlight close to or even on the ground, or patrolling their breeding territory. In woodlands where sunlit patches are at a premium, males defend these vigorously. Darker males patrol more vigorously than those with a paler wing colouration as they are able to regulate the optimum body temperature of around 33·5°C more efficiently.

HABITAT

Typically a common butterfly of woodland rides and glades, but can also be found along hedgerows and even in gardens.

POPULATION AND CONSERVATION

This species is extending its range, especially to the east, almost certainly in response to our changing climate. Numbers tend to increase following wet summers, but fall after drought years. This is a butterfly that has undergone several changes in status during the last 200 years, its latest resurgence starting in the 1920s.

WHERE TO FIN
In any suitable habita
within its range

OBSERVATION TIP
This butterfly can be see
on the wing in ever
month from April t
October, but is mos
abundant in late Augus
and early Septembe

Wall

Lasiommata megera

	Localised Resident
Wingspan:	45–53 m
Chrysalis:	16 m
Caterpillar:	24 m
Egg:	0·9 mm (

Though widely distributed, the Wall tends to be both localised and scarce. During the last 20 years it has been lost from many inland areas in both central and southern England, but has maintained its numbers on and around the coast and even expanded in more northerly areas.

IDENTIFICATION

ADULT : With its fast, flashing flight and golden upperwings this species suggests a fritillary or Comma. However, when seen at rest its bright 'eye' spots confirm its identity as a member of the brown family. The females are larger and brighter than the males. This is by far the most showy and active of all the British brown butterflies.

CHRYSALIS : Variable in colour from bright green to black, and attached to plant stems.

CATERPILLAR : Bluish-green, with white stripes.

EGG : Spherical, white, and laid singly or in clusters on a variety of grasses including bents and Yorkshire-fog.

BEHAVIOUR

The male spends much of his life patrolling in search of virgin females, pausing to feed on whatever flowers he passes. The gliding flight is fast and low. On cooler days, males spend much of their time basking in sunny, sheltered spots, such as south-facing walls (hence the name). The females are considerably less active.

HABITAT

A species that favours short, open grassland, where it is usually found on stony tracks, or where the turf is broken. It also likes coastal habitats, such as cliffs, as well as disturbed land, ranging from quarries to gardens.

POPULATION AND CONSERVATION

The loss of unimproved grassland has led to a marked decline in numbers inland, but the cause of its recent disappearance in parts of the south is not well understood. Its coastal populations seem to be doing well. This is a species that thrives in hot summers, and suffers in cool and damp conditions. There is evidence that it is expanding its range northwards.

WHERE TO FIN

Most easily locate around the coasts England and Wales, wher it tends to be mo abundant. Suitably sunr inland sites such as railwa embankments are alway worth checkin

OBSERVATION TIP

Most active on sunny day Basking males will ofte flush from tracks or path landing again a few metre in front of you, only t flush and land agai

Mountain Ringlet

Erebia epiphron

Our only true mountain butterfly, and restricted to the Scottish Highlands and the Lake District, where its fortunes fluctuate with the weather. It is one of our least-known butterflies.

Localised Resident

Wingspan:	male 28–36 m
	female 28–38 m
Chrysalis:	10–11 m
Caterpillar:	19–20 m
Egg:	1·2 mm (

IDENTIFICATION

ADULT : In Europe, identifying the numerous species of alpine ringlets is extremely difficult. Here we have just the single species, so identification is straightforward. This is the only brown butterfly likely to be found flying in its restricted mountain habitat. The orange spots are generally brighter on the female than the male. Mountain Ringlets in Scotland tend to be both brighter and bigger than those in the Lake District. The Scotch Argus (*page 132*), which occurs up to around 500 m, could be confused with this species. The Scotch Argus is, however, larger and brighter, and has distinctive white 'eye' spots on the upperside.

CHRYSALIS : Found in a loose cocoon at the base of the foodplant, Mat-grass.

CATERPILLAR : Green, with two yellowish stripes along the back, and a broader stripe along each side.

EGG : Barrel-shaped and ribbed, pale cream at first, becoming darker and mottled and then transparent. Laid singly on Mat-grass.

BEHAVIOUR

A sedentary, colonial species. On sunny days the males can be seen sunbathing or patrolling across their breeding grounds, always remaining close to the ground. Females rarely fly. The life-span is thought to be short, at the most just a few days.

HABITAT

Generally damp mountain grassland at altitudes of 500-700 m in the Lake District, and 350-900 m in Scotland. Scottish colonies favour south-facing slopes, but the Lake District colonies are more adaptable.

POPULATION AND CONSERVATION

Numbers appear to be stable, although it is possible that there are colonies in the Highlands that have yet to be discovered. The main threat to this species comes from over-grazing. Afforestation, and global warming are also possible threats.

WHERE TO FIN
Cumbria (Fleetwit
Honister Pass is the mo
accessible English colony
and central Scotlan
north of Ben Lomond an
between Fort William
the west, and th
Grampians in the eas

OBSERVATION TIP
With a short flight perio
and colony emergenc
depending on weathe
and altitude, this specie
can be easily overlooke
It is only worth looking fc
on warm, sunny day
when the males are active

Scotch Argus

Erebia aethiops

Though this butterfly flourishes throughout much of upland Scotland, it has declined in the southernmost parts of its range and can now only be found at two isolated sites in England.

Localised Resident

Wingspan:	male	44–48 m
	female	46–52 m
Chrysalis:		13 m
Caterpillar:		27 m
Egg:		1·3 mm (

IDENTIFICATION

ADULT : Most easily confused with the Meadow Brown (*page 140*), but this species is much darker (the upperwings of freshly emerged males are almost black), while the white 'eye' spots are distinctive. Unlike the Meadow Brown, the Scotch Argus only flies when the sun is shining. Usually found at lower altitudes than the smaller Mountain Ringlet (*page 130*).

CHRYSALIS : Difficult to find, formed at the base of grass tussocks.

CATERPILLAR : Ochreous, with two dark brown lines on the back, and a whitish band along each side.

EGG : Pale yellow, developing speckles with age. Extremely difficult to find in the wild, laid mainly on Purple Moor-grass in Scotland and Blue Moor-grass in England.

BEHAVIOUR

The males are most active in sunshine on windless days, when they will patrol incessantly in search of a mate, and make for cover as soon as the sun disappears. They are active as soon as the sun comes out, even very early in the morning on east-facing slopes. On overcast days, if the temperature is above 15°C, males may be moderately active. Flying males keep close to the ground, investigating anything that is brown. Females are inconspicuous, basking on sunny days and seldom taking flight.

HABITAT

In Scotland, this species is found in damp acid grasslands, around sheltered bogs and in woodland clearings, up to about 500m. The two English colonies are on sheltered limestone grassland.

POPULATION AND CONSERVATION

Stable in Scotland, where this butterfly is widespread and often abundant, though it is declining elsewhere in Europe. The chief threats to its survival are over-grazing, agricultural 'improvements' to grassland, and afforestation. The Cumbrian colonies are large and flourishing, but this butterfly once occurred at a number of other sites in northern England.

WHERE TO FIN

Colonies are easy t locate within its Scottis range, as this is often th commonest butterfly, ar present in great number

OBSERVATION TIP

Always look for th butterfly on sunny day The flight period relatively brief, the fir emergence is in the la week of July, but fe survive until Septembe

132

Marbled White

Melanargia galathea

This attractive and distinctive butterfly is widespread in southern England, and in recent years has been extending its range both northwards and eastwards.

IDENTIFICATION

ADULT : Though there are several very similar species to be found in southern Europe, in Britain there is no other species that can be confused with this black and white butterfly.

CHRYSALIS : Pale brown and unmarked, found under earth or moss at the surface of the ground.

CATERPILLAR : Pale brown or yellow, with two darkish lines along the back and a yellowish line along each side.

EGG : Spherical, pale green to white, and scattered near to the foodplants, usually fescue grasses.

BEHAVIOUR

A colonial species, sometimes to be found in large numbers. In the early morning and late afternoon, both sexes will sunbathe, perched on grass-heads or prominent flowers. In the heat of the day and in bright sunshine adults will feed with wings closed tightly. The slow, flapping flight of the Marbled White is distinctive.

HABITAT

Typically unimproved grassland, usually on chalk or limestone. They often occur on coastal grasslands, and may also be found on roadside verges or railway embankments.

POPULATION AND CONSERVATION

A butterfly that is increasing and extending its range, probably in response to warmer summers. It has shown an ability to make use of new habitats, such as fields of set-aside.

Widespread Residen

Wingspan:	male 53 r
	female 58 r
Chrysalis:	12–15 r
Caterpillar:	28 r
Egg:	1·0 mm

WHERE TO FIN

Most common in Dors Wiltshire, Somerset a Devon, and four wherever there is suitab habitat. Elsewhere in range it is more localise

OBSERVATION TIP

When sunbathing it highly approachable, takin little or no notice observers. The flig period is short, peaking mid-July, with numbe falling away sharply, so early August it h become quite scarc

Grayling

Hipparchia semele

Though the Grayling remains both widespread and reasonably common around the coast of Britain and Ireland, it has declined in many inland areas where it once flourished.

IDENTIFICATION

ADULT : Graylings almost invariably settle with their wings closed, so it is only when they are flying that one glimpses the broad yellow bands on the forewings of the female, or the dark sex brands on the forewings wing of the male. The underside of the hindwing is similar in both sexes, and provides perfect camouflage for the butterfly on bare ground.

CHRYSALIS : The brown chrysalis is formed below ground in a hollow lined with silk.

CATERPILLAR : Yellowish-white with a brown line along the back. It feeds at night.

EGG : The pale oval egg is strongly ribbed, and is laid singly on a wide variety of grasses growing in a sunny, open position.

BEHAVIOUR

This is a fast-flying species, often encountered when flushed from open ground, for example a stony path. The butterfly will fly rapidly ahead, with a distinctive gliding flight. As soon as it lands it shuts its wings, though the 'eye' spot on the underside of the forewing can be observed briefly before the butterfly draws its forewings out of sight. The female is secretive, so most sightings are of males. They are attracted to puddles, and when drinking, are easy to approach closely. In cool weather, Graylings spend a lot of time sunbathing, turning their bodies to catch the full warmth of the sun, while in hot sunshine they face the sun to minimise the sun's heat.

HABITAT

A colonial species usually found on coastal dunes or undercliffs. Inland colonies tend to be on dry heathland, chalk or limestone grassland, earthworks or in quarries. Its one essential requirement is dry, well-drained soil with lots of open ground.

POPULATION AND CONSERVATION

While most coastal colonies continue to flourish, this species has suffered from loss of habitat at many of its inland sites. Improved management of heathland may well help it to survive. However, this species is in overall decline, and its future seems uncertain.

Wingspan:	male	51–56m
	female	54–62mm
Chrysalis:		16mm
Caterpillar:		30m
Egg:		0·8mm (

WHERE TO FIND

Most easily located a coastal sites, particularly i southern and wester Britain or on heathland i southern England where can be abundan

OBSERVATION TIP

This species is most ofte flushed before it is seer Fortunately, it is attracte to the bare groun created by footpaths c wheel tracks, so is readil encountered

136

Gatekeeper

Pyronia tithonus

A widespread and highly successful species throughout the southern half of Britain. The Gatekeeper has also been extending its range northwards in recent years.

IDENTIFICATION

ADULT : Though often confused with the larger and duller Meadow Brown (*page 140*), this species is easy to identify thanks to its much brighter colouring, with its distinctive orange-on-chocolate on both the forewing and hindwing. Look, too, for the distinctive white dots on the underside of the hindwings (these are black on the Meadow Brown). The male is smaller and displays a broad band of dark scales (the sex-brand) on the forewing.

CHRYSALIS : Prettily marked, but hidden under a leaf, so rarely found in the wild.

CATERPILLAR : Hairy, colour variable, either light green-grey or pale yellow-brown, often speckled.

EGG : Spherical, white, mottling with age until becoming brown, laid on various grasses with fine leaves.

BEHAVIOUR

A colonial species, often found in abundance, though some colonies may be very small. The flight period is quite precise, starting in mid-July, peaking in early August, and all over by the end of that month. Gatekeepers are sedentary, and are rarely found far from their colony. They frequently sunbathe with wings open to the sun.

HABITAT

The alternative name of Hedge Brown gives a good indication of the favoured habitat, for this species is always associated with shrubs, so colonies are to be found along hedgerows or in scrubby woodland with plenty of wide and sunny rides.

POPULATION AND CONSERVATION

Common and widespread, but vulnerable to agricultural intensification and hedgerow removal.

Common Resident

Wingspan: male 37–43 m
female 42–48 m
Chrysalis: 12 m
Caterpillar: 25 m
Egg: 0·65 (w) × 0·65 mm

WHERE TO FIN
Readily found anywhere
suitable habitat in th
southern half of Britain
is extending its rang
northward

OBSERVATION TIF
This butterfly's habit
feeding and sunbathi
with open win
distinguishes at once fro
the Meadow Brow

Meadow Brown

Maniola jurtina

The familiar Meadow Brown is not only one of our most widespread butterflies, but often the most abundant, too. However, colonies are vulnerable to intensive farming, and the loss of the unimproved grassland they favour.

IDENTIFICATION

ADULT : The male is typically a dark, plain butterfly, his chocolate-brown wings relieved only by a tiny 'eye' spot in the corner of the forewing. The larger female has a bright orange blaze on the forewing. Old individuals are often heavily faded.

CHRYSALIS : Variable, sometimes brightly striped, but often simply plain green.

CATERPILLAR : Pale green above, darker below, with an off-white stripe along each side.

EGG : Almost spherical, ribbed and lightly spotted, and laid singly on the blades of a variety of grasses.

BEHAVIOUR

A slow-flying, meandering butterfly that seldom rises more than a metre above the ground. It will fly on dull days, even in light rain, when few other butterflies are active.

HABITAT

Typically a butterfly of open grasslands, but this is a highly adaptable and successful species, well able to adjust to a variety of different habitats where its foodplants can be found. Such habitats include roadside verges, woodland rides and urban habitats such as parks and cemeteries.

POPULATION AND CONSERVATION

A widespread and successful species, and the one recorded as most abundant according to results gathered by the Butterfly Monitoring Scheme. Colonies are, however, vulnerable to agricultural intensification.

Abundant Resident

Wingspan: male 40–50 mm
female 42–60 mm
Chrysalis: 16 mm
Caterpillar: 25 mm
Egg: 0·5 (w) × 0·5 mm

WHERE TO FIN
Almost anywhere
Britain and Ireland, exce
Shetlar

OBSERVATION TIP
Watch for a resting fema
raising her forewing
reveal the bright 'eye' sp
– a defence agair
predato

Ringlet
Aphantopus hyperantus

Widespread Resident

Wingspan: male 42–48 m
female 46–52 n
Chrysalis: 11–13 r
Caterpillar: 21 r
Egg: 0·8 (w) × 0·9mm

A widespread and successful species, and one that has been extending its range in both England and Scotland in recent years.

IDENTIFICATION

ADULT : Often confused with the Meadow Brown (*page 140*), from which it is readily separated by the bright, conspicuous 'eye' spots on the underside of the wing. The upperwing of a freshly emerged male is almost black, though this fades to brown with age. Females are slightly paler. Look out, too, for the distinctive white fringe to the wings. This species is prone to aberration, most noticeable in the 'eye' spots on the underwing ranging from *arete* **ar** with tiny white spots to *lanceolata* **la** with large, 'stretched' markings.

CHRYSALIS : Light sepia-brown, with darker markings, and hidden at the base of grass tussocks.

CATERPILLAR : Pale yellowish-brown, with a dark band along the back.

EGG : Dome-shaped, pale yellow, and scattered among coarse-leaved grasses.

BEHAVIOUR

Found in colonies of variable size, some numbering thousands of individuals. The distinctive bobbing flight is rather slow, but often undertaken on dull, cloudy days. Both sexes feed frequently on Bramble and thistle flowers.

HABITAT

Tall, lush grasslands, particularly in woodland rides and glades or around scrub and hedgerows. It favours heavy soils, while northern colonies tend to be in more open, less shady areas.

POPULATION AND CONSERVATION

This species is generally thriving, but tends to suffer badly following drought summers. It is vulnerable to over-grazing, while colonies can be encouraged by leaving grass rides and field headlands uncut.

WHERE TO FIN

Generally easy to fir
anywhere within its rang
but look for it in mo
shaded situations than tl
Meadow Brown, ar
especially along the edg
of woodlands or alor
ride

OBSERVATION TIP

Remember that the flig
period is relatively sho
and that following tl
peak flight period in tl
third week of Ju
numbers fall away quick

Small Heath
Coenonympha pamphilus

One of our most widespread butterflies, although many colonies have been lost in recent years due to intensive agriculture and changing patterns of land use.

Abundant Resident

Wingspan:	male 33 r
	female 37 r
Chrysalis:	8·5 r
Caterpillar:	20 r
Egg:	0·7mm

IDENTIFICATION

ADULT : Best identified by a combination of size, colour and behaviour. Its pale, washed-out beige colouring separates it from other brown butterflies, and from the four golden skippers (*pages 32-41*). The latter have a much quicker, darting flight.

Though not as variable as its larger cousin, the Large Heath, the Small Heath is also variable, with both bright and dull individuals flying together in the same colony. The size of the spots can also vary. Butterflies from western Scotland (sub-species *rhoumensis*) are usually the dullest.

CHRYSALIS : Green, usually with black streaking or stripes.

CATERPILLAR : Green, and well camouflaged, with a dark green, white-edged line along the back.

EGG : Almost spherical. Green, turning near-white and freckled, and laid singly on blades of fine-leaved grasses, especially Sheep's-fescue.

BEHAVIOUR

Its erratic, low flight is characteristic, while it never settles with its wings open. A perching Small Heath first lands with the 'eye' spot of the forewing visible, but soon afterwards the forewing is drawn within the hindwing. Males and unmated females congregate at leks where males fight amongst themselves to establish dominance prior to mating.

HABITAT

This species favours dry, well-drained grassland, particularly on heathland, downland or coastal dunes, but colonies may also be found in many other situations, from roadside verges to woodland rides. There is always a requirement for fine grasses which are the foodplant of the caterpillar.

POPULATION AND CONSERVATION

Though this butterfly flourishes where native grasses can be found in abundance, colonies are soon destroyed by so-called grassland 'improvement' and ploughing for arable crops. Light grazing is beneficial, but overgrazing can destroy the habitat. However, the decline of many colonies remains a mystery.

WHERE TO FIN

In suitable grassla habitat throughout mu of Britain and Ireland southern England adu may be encountered fro late April until even ea Octob

OBSERVATION TI

Adults like to sip nec from yellow flowers, su as dandelions a hawkbits. There are of aerial battles between ri males at territoral le

Large Heath

Coenonympha tullia

A butterfly of boggy moorland, the Large Heath remains widespread in parts of Ireland and over much of Scotland, but has declined severely in northern England and Wales.

IDENTIFICATION

ADULT : One of our most variable butterflies, with its appearance varying not only in different parts of its range, but also within colonies. Three forms have been recognised. In the far north, and on the Scottish islands, the form *scotica* **sco** occurs. This has pale, greyish wings that are virtually spotless. To the south, *polydama* **p** is typical. It is both slightly smaller and darker than *scotica*, with notable 'eye' spots. The third form, *davus*, **d** is perhaps the most attractive, with much redder wings and clearly pronounced 'eye' spots. This form is found in lowland England.

The only butterfly that the Large Heath can be confused with is the Small Heath, but the two are rarely, found together, for the former is a genuine wetland species, while the latter likes well-drained grassland.

CHRYSALIS : Green, with black stripes, though the boldness of the latter varies considerably.

CATERPILLAR : Green, with a yellow-edged dark green line along the back, and two prominent white bands along each side.

EGG : Almost spherical, yellow at first, developing dark blotches with age; laid on cottongrasses, favouring Hare's-tail Cottongrass.

BEHAVIOUR

A slow-flying and highly sedentary butterfly that can often be seen fluttering over bogs even on dull days. Like the Grayling, this butterfly never basks with its wings held open, but males will tilt their bodies to warm themselves in the sun.

HABITAT

Raised bogs, blanket bogs and acidic moorland, usually below 500 m. Its main requirements are Hare's-tail Cottongrass, the caterpillar's foodplant, and Cross-leaved Heath, a favourite source of nectar for the adults.

POPULATION AND CONSERVATION

With its specialised habitat vulnerable to afforestation, drainage, peat extraction and over-grazing, this is a highly sensitive species. Its future depends on safeguarding peatlands, and suitable management that includes protection from over-grazing.

Wingspan:	male 35–40 r
Chrysalis:	11 r
Caterpillar:	25 r
Egg:	0·8 mm

WHERE TO FIN

Easily found whe
suitable habitat remains
Scotland and Ireland;
main English stronghol
are in Northumberla
and Cumbr

OBSERVATION TIF

Though this butterfly v
fly on sunless days
avoids doing so when t
air temperature is belc
14°C, or when the wind
strong. Numbers usua
peak in mid-July, but t
most northerly coloni
may be up to a mon
behind those in the sou

VARIATIONS IN THE SILVER-WASHED FRITILLARY

The Silver-washed Fritillary form *valezina* (above) has a bronze-green base colour. This form occurs regularly in the forests of Hampshire, but rarely elsewhere. As much as one-tenth of the population may be of this form in some years. The Silver-washed Fritillary is also prone to melanism: one example is the aberrant form *ater* shown below.

Former breeding, occasional breeding and scarce migrant butterflies

The following plates show those species of butterfly that are not encountered annually in Britain.

FORMER BREEDING

LARGE COPPER

BLACK-VEINED WHITE

LARGE TORTOISESHELL

MAZARINE BLUE

This group comprises those species that no longer breed in Britain and which are regarded as extinct. There have been some efforts made to reintroduce these species with varying degrees of success, none of which has resulted in a population that is self-sustaining. Indeed, without the considerable efforts that have been made to understand the ecology of the Large Blue this, too, is a species that would be in this category.

The Large Tortoiseshell and Mazarine Blue occasionally reach Britain as migrants.

OCCASIONAL BREEDING

GERANIUM BRONZE

QUEEN OF SPAIN FRITILLARY

BERGER'S CLOUDED YELLOW

PALE CLOUDED YELLOW

BATH WHITE

This group contains those species which very occasionally reach our shores and may or may not breed. The Geranium Bronze is a species that may reach Britain on imported Geraniums from time to time and has bred. The Queen of Spain Fritillary has also bred. The Bath White and both of the rare clouded yellow species are thought to have bred in Britain. The true status of the clouded yellows is unknown, however, due to a combination of their extreme rarity and similarity to the Clouded Yellow.

SCARCE MIGRANT

CAMBERWELL BEAUTY

SHORT-TAILED BLUE

LONG-TAILED BLUE

MONARCH

This group contains those species which very occasionally reach our shores and have only ever been recorded as adults, although Long-tailed Blue caterpillars are sometimes imported with mange-tout peas. It is thought extremely unlikely that they could breed.

Large Copper
Lycaena dispar

Extinct in Britain for over 150 years, though successive unsuccessful reintroductions have been made until recently at Woodwalton Fen in Cambridgeshire.

IDENTIFICATION
ADULT : A stunningly eye-catching butterfly, both sexes readily identified by the brilliant copper-coloured wings that flash as they catch the sun. The male's wings are almost unmarked except for a black margin on the upperside; the female is larger and much more heavily marked. The undersides of both sexes are similar, the forewing being orange with black spots and the hindwing being silvery-grey with a blue suffusion and a prominent orange line near the rear margin. Readily told from the Small Copper by its larger size, and in the case of the male, its copper forewing and hindwing.

CHRYSALIS : Formed on the stem of Water Dock.

CATERPILLAR : Bright green.

EGG : Disc-shaped, laid singly on the leaves of Water Dock, the sole foodplant.

BEHAVIOUR
Lives in small colonies within extensive areas of habitat and only active on bright sunny days. Less pugnacious than the Small Copper, and the males are less territorial.

HABITAT
Open fen where the foodplant, Water Dock, flourishes.

STATUS
Always rare in England, its final extinction was due to the destruction of the extensive fenland habitat it requires. There are hopes that habitat management in the Norfolk Broads may allow this species to be reintroduced successfully, using stock from The Netherlands, where the single-brooded form is reduced to a single colony.

Extinct Resident	
Wingspan:	male 44–52 r
Chrysalis:	11 r
Caterpillar:	20 n
Egg:	0·65 (w) × 0·4mm

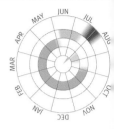

Distribution
Pre 1970

**WHERE IT WA
FOUN**
Woodwalton Fen was th
last site where th
butterfly could be see
but it is now thought th
this site is too small
support a viab
populatio

Black-veined White

Aporia crataegi

This handsome butterfly once had a highly localised distribution in southern England, but became extinct in the 1920s.

Extinct Resident

Wingspan:	56–68 m
Chrysalis:	25 m
Caterpillar:	34 m
Egg:	0·5 (w) × 1·0 mm (

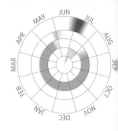

IDENTIFICATION

ADULT : A combination of size and its powerful soaring flight make this an easy butterfly to recognise. When perched, its beautifully veined wings are obvious and unmistakable.

CHRYSALIS : Variable, reflecting the location where it was formed, usually greenish-yellow spotted with black.

CATERPILLAR : Black with a broken ochre-coloured stripe on each flank.

EGG : Barrel-shaped, ribbed, primrose yellow when laid, turning grey over time.

Distribution
Pre 1900

BEHAVIOUR

A colonial species whose numbers tend to fluctuate wildly from year to year. Adults start the day by basking in the sun, before venturing out into the surrounding countryside. Both sexes spend much time feeding, when they are tame and readily approachable.

HABITAT

Scrub, woodland edge with Blackthorn and hawthorns, hay fields, roadside verges and orchards.

STATUS

Despite many attempts to re-establish this species in England, all have eventually failed. It remains widespread on the continent, though it has declined in many countries.

**WHERE IT WA
FOUN**

Its main strongholds wer
in southern Englan
although it extended as f
north as Yorkshir

Large Tortoiseshell
Nymphalis polychloros

Extinct Resident/Rare Migr[ant]	
Wingspan:	male 68–72 m
	female 72–75 m
Chrysalis:	27 m
Caterpillar:	40 m
Egg:	0.8 m

Many years have elapsed since this butterfly was recorded breeding in Britain and it is now almost certainly extinct. The few sightings every year are most likely to be of released individuals or sporadic migrants.

IDENTIFICATION

ADULT : This species resembles the Small Tortoiseshell (*page 104*) but is slightly larger and notably duller. The best way to tell the two apart is the complete absence of a white spot in the corner of the Large Tortoiseshell's forewing.

CHRYSALIS : Variable in colour, but usually well camouflaged.

CATERPILLAR : Black body, with minute white spots and orange stripe on either side, and with orange-brown spines. Gregarious, feeding beneath an obvious silken web.

EGG : The eggs are laid in batches encircling twigs of elm or willow. They start yellow, and become darker with age.

BEHAVIOUR

Large Tortoiseshells fly for only a week or so in July before hibernating, seeking out cracks or holes in tree trunks. They emerge the following spring, when they can often be found basking, with wings held wide apart, on tree trunks that have been warmed by the sun. They are fast, strong fliers. Mating takes place in early April, and by the end of that month few, if any, adults survive.

HABITAT

A butterfly that favours the edge of deciduous woodlands, but can also be found in well-wooded hedgerows, or even avenues of trees. Emerging adults like to feed on willows, so favoured woodlands usually have an abundance of these tree species.

STATUS

Though it is often suggested that migrants from the Continent reach southern England, these seem to be so infrequent that there is little chance of this species re-establishing itself naturally in Britain. Its population has risen and fallen in the past, but its last period of abundance in England was 1945–48. Many recent sightings have been traced to releases of captive stock, but the numerous sightings along the south and east coast of England are generally considered to be migrants.

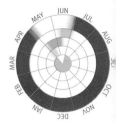

Distribution
Pre 1970

WHERE IT WA[S] FOUN[D]

Though its stronghold wa[s] southern England, th[is] butterfly once occurred [in] the Midlands, and ha[s] been recorded from bot[h] Scotland and Wales. An[y] sightings of this species [in] the wild should b[e] reported at onc[e]

Geranium Bronze

Cacyreus marshalli

A southern African species, now firmly established in several Mediterranean countries, and recently recorded in England.

Introduced?

Wingspan: male 15–23 m
female 18–27 m
Chrysalis: 13 m
Caterpillar: 9 m
Egg: 0·5 (w) × 0·3 mm (

IDENTIFICATION

ADULT : Tiny. Look for the distinctive tails on the hindwings, and the chequered white fringe to the upperside of both the forewings and hindwings, which are, indeed, bronze-coloured. The underside of both the forewings and hindwings are heavily patterned. There is no other, native, species that this butterfly can be confused with.

CHRYSALIS : Can be found either attached to the host plant or in leaf-litter on the ground.

CATERPILLAR : Green and hairy.

EGG : Laid singly on flower buds or the underside of cultivated geraniums.

BEHAVIOUR

A weak-flying species, usually found close to its favoured foodplant. It first succeeded in colonising the Balearic Islands, and then coastal Mediterranean Spain, as a result of being accidentally imported (probably as caterpillars) with geranium plants.

HABITAT

In Europe it depends on cultivated geraniums, so is invariably found in gardens, window boxes or wherever its foodplants can be found. It requires warm winters for its survival, so is unlikely to become established in Britain.

STATUS

An unwelcome colonist in the Mediterranean, where its caterpillar's liking for the leaves, stems and flowers of geraniums has made it unpopular with gardeners. It has already proved to be a serious pest in the horticultural trade and is designated as a 'pest species'. Sightings in the UK should be reported to the Plant Health Service (*page 183*).

WHERE TO FIN
The only British recorc so far have been in Susse in 1997 and 1998, an Cambridgshire i December 2001 bu more sightings are likel

OBSERVATION TIP
Geraniums with heavy lea damage may indicate tha this species is presen

Queen of Spain Fritillary

Issoria lathonia

A rare migrant from the near continent, but one that might have bred recently in eastern England.

Rare Migrant

Wingspan: male 34–52 m
female 50–56 m
Chrysalis: 17–19 m
Caterpillar: 32 m
Egg: 0·65 mm (

IDENTIFICATION

ADULT : The distinctive wing shape and fast, powerful flight give this species a totally different jizz from any of our other fritillaries. The best distinguishing marks, however, are the large silver patches on the underside of the hindwings. The female is larger than the male, and has similar silver patches on the hindwings, though with a touch of green at the base.

CHRYSALIS : Olive-brown with white markings, and resembles a bird's dropping.

CATERPILLAR : Variable, usually velvety black speckled with white.

EGG : Pale, conical and laid singly on, probably, Wild Pansy or Field Pansy, although many species of violets are used in continental Europe.

BEHAVIOUR

A low-flying, sun-loving species that often stops to bask in the sun, usually on bare patches of ground where it will perch with wings held open in a wide V, aimed towards the sun. Though a strong flyer, there is a slight jerkiness that is reminiscent of the Wall (*page 128*). This species lives in residential colonies on the continent, from which some individuals may wander considerable distances.

HABITAT

A rare migrant to southern England, so can be encountered anywhere. On the continent it favours dry limestone areas, heathland and sand dunes where its favoured foodplant, the Field Pansy, grows commonly. The nearest colonies to Britain are in The Netherlands, in dunes along the North Sea coast.

STATUS

In the late 1990s there were a number of records on the Suffolk coast that suggested that a small temporary breeding colony might have become established in Britain. It is widely distributed and often quite common on the continent. Otherwise, migrants may be encountered anywhere along the south coast, especially in the autumn.

WHERE TO FIN[

Look for this species o
the coast of East Angli
Do not expect succes
Migrants may b
encountered anywher
along the south coas

WHEN TO LOO[

Adults are normal
encountered [
September and Octobe
A few sightings have bee
made between the end o
May and Augus

Berger's Clouded Yellow

Colias alfacariens

A very rare visitor to southern England, very similar to the Pale Clouded Yellow, so its true status is unknown.

Rare Migrant		
Wingspan:	male	50–56 m
	female	50–60 n
Chrysalis:		22 m
Caterpillar:		32 n
Egg:		1·1 mm

IDENTIFICATION: ADULT : Both sexes are very similar to the Pale Clouded Yellow, and cannot be separated without difficulty in the field. However, males of this species are usually more intensely coloured, the orange spot on the hindwing is brighter, and the dark markings less distinct. More likely to be found on downland than Pale Clouded Yellow. None of the stages are thought to be able to survive the winter (see also Clouded Yellow (*page 52*).
CHRYSALIS : Plain, bright green; darkening with age.
CATERPILLAR : Turquoise-blue with black spots and two yellow stripes. EGG : Laid singly on the foodplant.

BEHAVIOUR: All three species of clouded yellow are similar in their behaviour, always landing with their wings shut. This is a more active butterfly than the Pale Clouded Yellow, although it is thought to be less likely to migrate any distance.

HABITAT: The foodplant of this species is Horseshoe Vetch, and this dictates where this species may be found – typically on open chalk downland.

STATUS: The status of this species is uncertain, owing to its similarity to the Pale Cloude Yellow and *helice* Clouded Yellow. It was only recognised as a separate species in 1947.

WHERE TO FIN
Downland, or cliff tops
Kent or Sussex, but only
you are extremely luc
Check areas whe
Horseshoe Vetch is foun

WHEN TO LOO
Rarely in May and Jun
most frequent in Augu
and early Septembe
occasionally in Octob

Pale Clouded Yellow

Colias hya

A very rare visitor to southern England, though it may have bred here in the past.

Rare Migrant		
Wingspan:	male	52–56 m
	female	52–62 m
Chrysalis:		22 m
Caterpillar:		32 m
Egg:		1·0 mm

IDENTIFICATION: ADULT : The male is a distinctive lemon-yellow, so should not be confused with any other species except Berger's Clouded Yellow. Look for its more pointed forewings and more extensive black edges to the hindwings than Clouded Yellow (*page 52*). The female is much paler, almost white, and is very similar to *helice* Clouded Yellow, and also to female Berger's Clouded Yellow. The upperside of the hindwings lack the grey suffusion of *helice*, while Berger's tends to be paler still.
CHRYSALIS : Very similar in colouring and appearance to Clouded Yellow but with a pale red stripe on the back. CATERPILLAR : Green, finely speckled with black, and with a white line along either flank.
EGG : Laid singly on the foodplant, usually clovers or Lucerne.

BEHAVIOUR: Very similar to Clouded Yellow: a fast, low-flying butterfly that always lands with its wings shut. This species is regarded as less migratory than the Clouded Yellow.

HABITAT: Catholic in its choice of habitat, but typically found in cultivated meadows where its foodplants, Lucerne and clover, can be found.

STATUS: A rare vagrant to southern England, though it may have bred here in 1947 aft the last major immigration. There may be several years between reported occurrences.

WHERE TO FIN
Migrants are best looke
for in clover-rich meadow
close to the Chann
coast of southern Englan

WHEN TO LOO
May and June, and aga
in August and ear
Septembe

Ad

Ca

Ad

Ca

Ch

Berger's Clouded Yellow

M

F

Pale Clouded Yellow

M

F

F

Clouded Yellow (*page 52*)

hel

M

The uppersides of
clouded yellows are
normally only seen in
flight. A good view is
essential to the
identification of these
similar species.

Bath White

Pontia daplidi

A very rare visitor to southern England, though it may have bred here in the past.

Rare Migrant	
Wingspan:	19–24 m
Chrysalis:	19 n
Caterpillar:	25 m
Egg:	0·85 mm

IDENTIFICATION: ADULT : In flight, a Bath White can easily be mistaken for a Green-veined (*page 60*) or Small White(*page 58*), despite its more purposeful flight. At rest, the mottled pattern and colour of the underside of the hindwing is easily confused with the female Orange-tip (*page 62*), although during the spring flight period of this species the Bath White is highly unlikely to be encountered in England. Seen well, the black-and-white chequering of the upper wing-tips of the Bath White is diagnostic. CHRYSALIS : Pale grey. CATERPILLAR : Lilac-grey with yellow stripes. EGG : Long, thin and pale yellow.

BEHAVIOUR: A very mobile species, flying great distances.

HABITAT: Adults can be seen almost anywhere, often found on derelict, disturbed ground or rough land and roadside verges.

WHERE TO FIN
Anywhere in southe
Englar

WHEN TO LOO
Late July and August a
the months in which th
species is most likely to k
encountere

STATUS: In 1945 there was an exceptional immigration to southern England, and the species almost certainly bred here. Subsequent records have be few. On the continent it is a migratory species, moving northwards and colonising new are breeding for a few generations and then usually dying out as it is generally unable to survi northern European winters.

Camberwell Beauty

Nymphalis antio

A rare but regular vagrant from the continent and Scandinavia that has never been recorded breeding in Britain.

Annual Migrant	
Wingspan:	60–65 m

IDENTIFICATION: ADULT : Readily identified by its large size, deep chocolate-brown wings fringed with pale yellow (sometimes almost white) borders, and a line of blue dots edging these margins. The underside is dark, but the pale margin can be seen. This is a long-lived species, and towards the end of the flight period specimens are often very tatty and faded.

BEHAVIOUR: Its powerful flight is similar to that of a Red Admiral and, like this species, it will readily come to gardens and feed on buddleias. This species hibernates as an adult, the adults emerging in early spring. It seems likely that spring records in Britain are of individuals that have over-wintered successfully.

WHERE TO FIN
Almost anywhere in th
UK, although there is
bias towards East Ang
and south-east Englan

WHEN TO LOO
Most likely to be seen
late summer/early autum
although it has be
recorded in every mont

HABITAT: In Scandinavia and continental Europe this species is usually found in or near woodland. Camberwell Beauties in Britain have been seen in a variety of habitats, including sand dunes, parks and gardens, especially feeding on buddleias. The first British records were of two seen in Camberwell, south London, in 1748.

STATUS: A widespread species on the continent, recorded annually in Britain. Exception influxes to Britain occur occasionally, such as in 1995 when some 350 sightings were reporte

Short-tailed Blue

Cupido argiad[es]

An extremely rare vagrant to southern England. The first British specimens were recorded at Bloxworth Heath in Dorset.

Rare Vagrant

Wingspan: 20–30 m[m]

IDENTIFICATION: ADULT : One of a number of similar species that occur in Europe. The tails are tiny but distinctive. Look also for the twin orange spots near the tail on the underside which separates this from all the other blues, including the other short-tailed blues that occur on the continent. The male has violet-blue wings with black margins, while the female is dark brown with purple scales near the base of the wings.

BEHAVIOUR: Unlike the Long-tailed Blue, this is a non-migratory species, only rarely wandering to southern England. On the continent it is most active in the early morning and late afternoon, resting during the heat of the day.

HABITAT: Woodland edges, unimproved grassland and heaths.

STATUS: Only recorded as an adult in Britain. The Short-tailed Blue is extending its range on the continent, so with climate change could potentially colonise southern England as it utilises a range of foodplants in the p[ea] family, including Common Bird's-foot-trefoil, Red Clover and Tufted Vetch, which are comm[on] in Britain.

WHERE TO FIN[D]
The most likely locatio[n] for this extremely ra[re] butterfly are clover-ri[ch] fields along the sou[th] coa[st]

WHEN TO LOO[K]
July-September, especial[ly] after periods of souther[n] wind[s]

Long-tailed Blue

Lampides boetic[us]

A migratory butterfly that is a rare and irregular visitor to southern England.

Rare Migrant

Wingspan: male 32–34 m[m]
female 36-42 m[m]

IDENTIFICATION: ADULT : Most easily identified by the distinctive tails on the trailing edge of the hindwing (though these can become broken), with two adjacent black spots. Look also for the distinctive white striping on the underside of both the hindwings and forewings. The upperside of the male is violet-blue, while the female is predominantly brown with variable amounts of blue scales. CHRYSALIS : Pale pink with brown blotches, becoming cream-coloured with age.
CATERPILLAR : Dark green, becoming russet-brown with age.
EGG : Almost spherical, creamy-white.

BEHAVIOUR: A fast-flying butterfly whose strong flight is similar to that of a hairstreak. When feeding it has a characteristic rapid, jerky flight which is very different from any similar species.

HABITAT: On the continent, most often found in flower-rich meadows. Most British recor[ds] have been in gardens, or on downland in the southern third of England.

STATUS: A highly successful and widespread species, and often abundant within its rang[e]. The British climate is too cool for it to become established here. This is a highly migrato[ry] species that often irrupts north from southern Europe, but rarely crosses the English Channe[l]. Caterpillars are occasionally found in imported Mange-tout peas.

WHERE TO FIN[D]
In gardens along the sou[th] coast or on downlan[d] with other blue[s]

WHEN TO LOO[K]
Most sightings are [in] August and Septemb[er]

Mazarine Blue

Polyommatus semiargr

A little-known former resident of England that became extinct around 1903, now a very rare accidental visitor.

Extinct Resident/Vagran

Wingspan: male 32–36 m
female 34–38 m

IDENTIFICATION: ADULT: The upperside of the male Mazarine Blue is a dull purplish-blue; the female is brown. Both sexes have a narrow black margin with white edges to the wings. The underside is pale brown with a blue tinge near the body and a few black spots encircled with white. Only the Silver-studded Blue (*page 78*) has a similar upperwing colouration but is identified by the silver-blue centred black spots on the underside of the hindwing.

BEHAVIOUR: Lives in discrete colonies in Europe and is generally non-migratory.

HABITAT: Unimproved pasture and hay meadows where its main foodplant, Red Clover, occurs.

STATUS: Now extinct in Britain, with few records of genuine immigrants from the south coast of England. Its distribution in England and reasons for its extinction are not fully known.

WHERE TO FIN
There is little chance
seeing a Mazarine Blue
Britain; the few moder
records have been fro
the south coast. Fiel
with Red Clover may off
the best sliver of hop
WHEN TO LOO
Most records of migran
come from June and Ju

Monarch

Danaus plexippr

A rare but regular migrant from North America, especially to south-west Britain and Ireland.

Rare Vagrant

Wingspan: 105–112 m

IDENTIFICATION: ADULT: Unmistakable. The combination of its large size (much the largest butterfly to occur naturally in Britain) and its conspicuous and distinctive colouring ensures that the Monarch can be recognised instantly, even by people with little knowledge of butterflies. The male and female are very similar, and both have the same stately, almost bird-like flight.

BEHAVIOUR: A very strong flyer and most likely to be seen soaring rapidly searching for nectar plants. When feeding it can be very approachable.

HABITAT: Found in a wide range of habitats in North America, but in Britain generally found close to the coast, often in gardens.

STATUS: A highly migratory and long-lived butterfly that is widespread in North America. In the autumn, Monarchs migrate south to their winter roosts in California and Mexico, and it is at this time that wind-blown vagrants regularly reach Britain: most records are in September and October. In 1999, a record number of over 300 individuals was recorded in Britain. Monarchs have become reasonably well established in the Canary Islands and Spain, although it is more likely that those reaching our shores are from America. There is no suitable breeding habitat for the species in Britain, as foodplants of the milkweed family do not occur.

WHERE TO FIN
In areas rich with nect
plants, including gardens,
the south and west
Britain and usually ne
the coa
There are regular autum
sightings in the Isles
Sci
WHEN TO LOO
September and Octob
after stormy depression
have crossed the Atlant

Eggs, caterpillars and chrysali

Pages 169-178 show the eggs, caterpillars and chrysali of all Britain's breeding species.

The eggs are depicted at 10× life size and each photograph has a scale rule line.
Caterpillars and chrysali are all depicted at actual size. The photographs are the same as those depicted in the plates, but are collated together for ease of reference. A rule is given on each page to help gauge the size of any caterpillars or chrysali encountered in the wild.

Chequered Skipper

Small Skipper

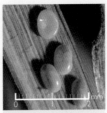

Essex Skipper

Lulworth Skipper

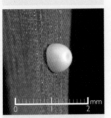

Silver-spotted Skipper

Large Skipper

Dingy Skipper

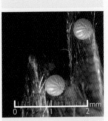

Grizzled Skipper

Wood White

Clouded Yellow

Brimstone

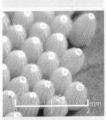

Large White (cluster)

Small White

Green-veined White

Orange Tip

Green Hairstreak

Brown Hairstreak

Purple Hairstreak

White-letter Hairstreak

Black Hairstreak

Eggs – 10 × Life size

169

Small Copper

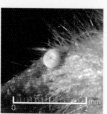

Small Blue

Silver-studded Blue

Brown Argus

Northern Brown Argus

Common Blue

Chalkhill Blue

Adonis Blue

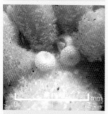

Holly Blue

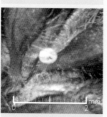

Large Blue

Duke of Burgundy

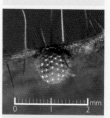

White Admiral

Purple Emperor

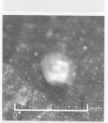

Red Admiral

Painted Lady

Small Tortoiseshell
(cluster)

Peacock
(cluster)

Comma

Small Pearl-
bordered Fritillary

Pearl-bordered
Fritillary

High Brown
Fritillary

Dark Green
Fritillary

Silver-washed
Fritillary

Marsh Fritillary
(cluster)

Glanville Fritillary
(cluster)

Heath Fritillary
(cluster)

Speckled Wood

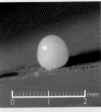

Wall

Mountain Ringlet

Scotch Argus

Marbled White

Grayling

Gatekeeper

Meadow Brown

Ringlet

Small Heath

Large Heath

Swallowtail

Eggs – 10 × Life size

171

 Chequered Skipper

 Small Skipper

 Essex Skipper

 Lulworth Skipper

 Silver-spotted Skipper

 Large Skipper

 Dingy Skipper

 Grizzled Skipper

 Wood White

 Clouded Yellow

 Brimstone

 Small White

 Green-veined White

 Orange Tip

Large White

 Brown Hairstreak

Purple Hairstreak

 White-letter Hairstreak

Black Hairstreak

172

Green Hairstreak

Small Copper

Small Blue

Silver-studded Blue

Brown Argus

Northern Brown Argus

Common Blue

Chalkhill Blue

Adonis Blue

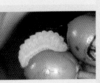

Holly Blue

Large Blue

Duke of Burgundy

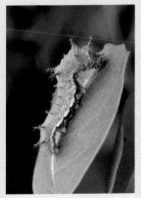

White Admiral

Purple Emperor

Peacock

Red Admiral

Small Tortoiseshell

Comma

Caterpillars – Life size

173

Painted Lady

Small Pearl-
bordered Fritillary

Pearl-bordered
Fritillary

Marsh Fritillary

High Brown Fritillary

Dark Green Fritillary

Silver-washed Fritillary

Glanville Fritillary

Heath Fritillary

Speckled Wood

Wall

Mountain Ringlet

Scotch Argus

Marbled White

Grayling

174

Swallowtail

Gatekeeper

Meadow Brown

Large Heath

Ringlet

Small Heath

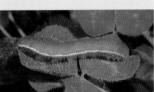

Pale Clouded Yellow

Large Tortoiseshell

Queen of Spain Fritillary

Berger's Clouded Yellow

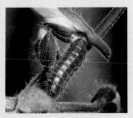

Geranium Bronze

Bath White

Black-veined White

mm

Caterpillars – Life size

175

Chequered Skipper

Small Skipper

Essex Skipper

Lulworth Skipper

Silver-spotted Skipper

Large Skipper

Dingy Skipper

Grizzled Skipper

Wood White

Clouded Yellow

Brimstone

Large White

Small White

Green-veined White

Orange Tip

Green Hairstreak

Brown Hairstreak

Purple Hairstreak

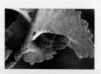
White-letter Hairstreak

Black Hairstreak

Small Copper

Small Blue

Silver-studded Blue

Brown Argus

Northern Brown
Argus

Common Blue

Chalkhill Blue

Adonis Blue

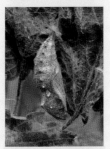

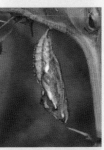

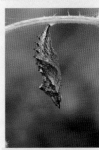

Holly Blue

Large Blue

Duke of Burgundy

White Admiral

Purple Emperor

Red Admiral

Painted Lady

Small Tortoiseshell

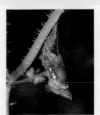

Peacock

Comma

Small Pearl-
bordered Fritillary

Pearl-bordered
Fritillary

Chrysali – Life size

177

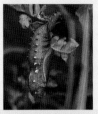

High Brown
Fritillary

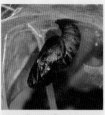

Dark Green
Fritillary

Silver-washed
Fritillary

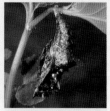

Marsh Fritillary

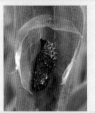

Glanville Fritillary

Heath Fritillary

Speckled Wood

Wall

Mountain Ringlet

Scotch Argus

Marbled White

Grayling

Gatekeeper

Meadow Brown

Ringlet

Small Heath

Large Heath

Swallowtail

Butterfly food sources and caterpillar foodplants

The requirements of adult butterflies are usually vastly different from those of the caterpillar. Adults require nectar-rich plants in flower, and caterpillars require succulent vegetative matter. Whilst adults of many species are cosmopolitan in their choice of food sources, some are not; caterpillars tend to be very specific in their requirements.

This table shows what are recognised as the most important sources of food for both adults and caterpillars. **Bold text** indicates that the food source is one upon which the species is wholly or very largely dependent. *Italicised text* is used to highlight those food sources that are non-specific. Green text is used to highlight any additional information of importance that is unrelated to the food sources.

BUTTERFLY	ADULT FOOD SOURCE	CATERPILLAR FOODPLANT
ADONIS BLUE *Lysandra bellargus*	Bramble, eyebrights, Horseshoe Vetch, Wild Marjoram, knapweeds, scabious, thistles	**Horsehoe Vetch**. Attended by the ants *Lasius alienus, Myrmica sabuleti*
BLACK HAIRSTREAK *Satyrium pruni*	**Aphid honeydew**, Blackthorn, Wild Privet	**Blackthorn**
BRIMSTONE *Gonepteryx rhamni*	*Purple and mauve flowers*	Buckthorn, Alder Buckthorn
BROWN ARGUS *Aricia agestis*	Common Rock-rose; *wide variety of downland plants*	Common Rock-rose, Common Stork's-bill, Dove's-foot Crane's-bill. Often attended by *Lasius alienus, Myrmica sabuleti*
BROWN HAIRSTREAK *Thecla betulae*	**Aphid honeydew**, Common Fleabane, thistles, Bramble	**Blackthorn**
CHALKHILL BLUE *Lysandra coridon*	*Wide variety of chalk downland plants*	**Horsehoe Vetch**
CHEQUERED SKIPPER *Carterocephalus palaemon*	Bluebell, Bugle, Marsh Thistle	Purple Moor-grass (Scotland), False Brome (England)
COMMA *Polygonia c-album*	*Wide variety*	Currants, elms, Hop, Common Nettle, willows
COMMON BLUE *Polyommatus icarus*	*Wide variety*	**Common Bird's-foot-trefoil**. Attended by the ants *Formica rufa, Myrmica sabuleti*
DARK GREEN FRITILLARY *Argynnis aglaja*	Knapweeds, Red Clover, thistles; *purple and mauve flowers*	Hairy Violet, Marsh Violet, Common Dog-violet
DINGY SKIPPER *Erynnis tages*	*Various but especially* Common Bird's-foot-trefoil	Common Bird's-foot-trefoil, Greater Bird's-foot-trefoil
DUKE OF BURGUNDY *Hamearis lucina*	*Chalk downland plants in flower*	Cowslip, Primrose
ESSEX SKIPPER *Thymelicus lineola*	Field Scabious, Red Clover, thistles	Cock's-foot, Common Couch, Creeping Soft-grass, Timothy
GATEKEEPER *Pyronia tithonus*	Bramble, Common Fleabane, ragworts	Bents, fescues
GLANVILLE FRITILLARY *Melitaea cinxia*	Thrift; *assorted yellow flowers*	**Ribwort Plantain**

BUTTERFLY	ADULT FOOD SOURCE	CATERPILLAR FOODPLANT
GRAYLING *Hipparchia semele*	*Heathland plants in flower*	Bristle Bent, Early Hair-grass, fescues, Marram, Tufted Hair-grass
GREEN HAIRSTREAK *Callophrys rubi*	Hawkweeds, hawthorns	Common Rock-rose, Common Bird's-foot-trefoil, Broom, Gorse, Dogwood, Bilberry
GREEN-VEINED WHITE *Pieris napi*	*Wide variety*	Charlock, Cuckooflower, Garlic Mustard, Water-cress
GRIZZLED SKIPPER *Pyrgus malvae*	Common Bird's-foot-trefoil, buttercups, Compositae	Wild Strawberry, Silverweed, Tormentil, Creeping Cinquefoil
HEATH FRITILLARY *Mellicta athalia*	Bramble	Common Cow-wheat, Ribwort Plantain, Germander Speedwell *(depending on location)*
HIGH BROWN FRITILLARY *Argynnis adippe*	Bramble, thistles	**Common Dog-violet**
HOLLY BLUE *Celastrina argiolus*	Bramble, forget-me-nots, Holly	Holly (spring), Ivy (summer)
LARGE BLUE *Maculinea arion*	*Chalk downland plants in flower*	**Wild Thyme**. Later in nests of the ant *Myrmica sabuleti*
LARGE HEATH *Coenonympha tullia*	Cross-leaved Heath; *blanket bog plants in flower*	**Hare's-tail Cottongrass**
LARGE SKIPPER *Ochlodes venata*	Bramble, thistles	Cock's-foot, False Brome
LARGE TORTOISESHELL *Nymphalis polychloros*	Willows (Spring); *wide variety* (Summer)	Elms, willows
LARGE WHITE *Pieris brassicae*	*Wide variety*	Brassicas, Wild Mignonette
LULWORTH SKIPPER *Thymelicus acteon*	Ragworts, Bramble, Wild Marjoram, Restharrow, thistles	**Tor-grass**
MARBLED WHITE *Melanargia galathea*	Knapweeds, scabious, thistles	Red Fescue, Sheep's-fescue
MARSH FRITILLARY *Eurodryas aurinia*	Betony, buttercups, Tormentil Marsh Thistle	**Devil's-bit Scabious**
MEADOW BROWN *Maniola jurtina*	Thistles, *wide variety*	Bents, meadow-grasses
NORTHERN BROWN ARGUS *Aricia artaxerxes*	*Limestone plants in flower*	**Common Rock-rose**
ORANGE-TIP *Anthocharis cardamines*	Bugle, Cruciferae	Cuckooflower, Garlic Mustard; *wide range of Cruciferae*
PAINTED LADY *Cynthia cardui*	*Wide variety*	Thistles
PEACOCK *Inachis io*	Buddleias, Hemp-agrimony, teasels; *wide variety*	**Common Nettle**
PEARL-BORDERED FRITILLARY *Boloria euphrosyne*	Bluebell, Bugle; *wide variety*	Common Dog-violet, Marsh Violet

BUTTERFLY	ADULT FOOD SOURCE	CATERPILLAR FOODPLANT
PURPLE EMPEROR *Apatura iris*	**Aphid honeydew on oaks**	Goat Willow, Grey Willow
PURPLE HAIRSTREAK *Quercusia quercus*	**Aphid honeydew on oaks**	**Oak**
RED ADMIRAL *Vanessa atalanta*	*Wide variety*	**Common Nettle**
RINGLET *Aphantopus hyperantus*	Bramble, Compositae	*Variety of coarse grasses, eg* Cock's-foot, Common Couch
SCOTCH ARGUS *Erebia aethiops*	*Upland bog plants in flower*	Purple Moor-grass (Scotland), Blue Moor-grass (England)
SILVER-SPOTTED SKIPPER *Hesperia comma*	Field scabious, Red Clover, thistles	**Sheep's-fescue**
SILVER-STUDDED BLUE *Plebejus argus*	*Heathland plants in flower*	Bird's-foot-trefoil, vetches, heaths Attended by the ant *Lasius alienus*
SILVER-WASHED FRITILLARY *Argynnis paphia*	Honeydew, Bramble, thistles	Common Dog-violet, Marsh Violet
SMALL BLUE *Cupido minimus*	Common Bird's-foot-trefoil, Kidney Vetch, Horseshoe Vetch	**Kidney Vetch**
SMALL COPPER *Lycaena phlaes*	Compositae	Common Sorrel, Sheep's Sorrel
SMALL HEATH *Coenonympha pamphilus*	*Wide variety*	Bents, Fescues
SMALL MOUNTAIN RINGLET *Erebia epiphron*	Tormentil; *moorland plants in* *flower*	**Mat-grass**
SMALL PEARL-BORDERED FRITILLARY *Boloria selene*	Common Bird's-foot-trefoil, Bluebell, Ragged-Robin	Common Dog-violet, Marsh Violet
SMALL SKIPPER *Thymelicus sylvestris*	Field Scabious, Red Clover, thistles	Yorkshire-fog, Creeping Soft- grass, Timothy
SMALL TORTOISESHELL *Aglais urticae*	*Wide variety*	**Common Nettle**
SMALL WHITE *Pieris rapae*	*Wide variety*	Brassicas, Cruciferae
SPECKLED WOOD *Pararge aegeria*	**Aphid honeydew on Ash,** **birches, oaks**; ragworts	Cock's-foot, False Brome, Yorkshire-fog
SWALLOWTAIL *Papilio machaon*	Milk-parsley	**Milk-parsley**
WALL *Lasiommata megera*	*Wide variety*	Cock's-foot, Tor-grass, Wavy Hair-grass, Yorkshire-fog
WHITE ADMIRAL *Ladoga camilla*	Aphid honeydew on oaks, Bramble	**Honeysuckle**
WHITE-LETTER HAIRSTREAK *Satyrium w-album*	**Aphid honeydew on elms**, Bramble, Creeping Thistle	English Elm, Small-leaved Elm, Wych Elm
WOOD WHITE *Leptidea sinapis*	*Woodland plants in flower*	Meadow Vetchling, Tufted Vetch, Common Bird's-foot-trefoil

Glossary

Culm grasslands   Species-rich grassland occurring on the Culm Measures in south-west England.

Family   A unit of taxonomic classification comprising an assemblage of genera considered to be closely related due to shared characters.

Genus   A unit of taxonomic classification comprising a number of species that are more closely related to one another than to other species in other genera.

Hibernation   The dormant stage in which an animal passes the winter.

Jizz   The often indefinable characteristic impression given by an animal or plant.

Lek   A communal 'display' ground where males congregate to attract and court females, and to which females come for mating.

Migrant   A species that undertakes periodic movements to or from a given area, usually along well-defined routes and at predictable times of the year.

Nectaring   Feeding on nectar.

NNR   National Nature Reserve.

RSPB   The Royal Society for the Protection of Birds.

Sex-brand   A grouping of specialised wing-scales in male butterflies, that possess gland cells which contain special chemicals (pheromones) for attracting females. These often form conspicuous patches in the upperside of the forewing.

Species   The basic unit of taxonomic classification that relates to a group of individuals of an organism that is capable of interbreeding and producing viable offspring.

Spiracles   External respiratory openings.

Vagrant   An individual that wanders outside the normal range of the species.

Further reading

Anyone whose interest in butterflies has been aroused by this book should buy a copy of *The Millennium Atlas of Butterflies in Britain and Ireland*. Produced by Butterfly Conservation, in conjunction with the Biological Records Centre and The Dublin Naturalists' Field Club, and published by Oxford University Press, it is not only a beautiful book to browse through, but also an outstanding and authoritative work of reference. The text is by Jim Asher, Martin Warren, Richard Fox, Paul Harding, Gail Jeffcoate and Stephen Jeffcoate.

Quite the most readable book on Britain's butterflies to have been produced in the last 50 years is *The Butterflies of Britain & Ireland* (National Trust/Dorling Kindersley). Nobody knows Britain's butterflies better than its author, Dr Jeremy Thomas, and his essays on each species are a delight. The illustrations are by Richard Lewington, Britain's leading butterfly artist.

As a comprehensive guide to Europe's butterflies, the *Collins Field Guide: Butterflies of Britain & Europe*, with text by Tom Tolman and illustrations by Richard Lewington, is quite outstanding. It covers over 440 species, with over 2,000 colour illustrations.

Also highly recommended is *The Pocket Guide to Butterflies of Britain and Europe*, published by Mitchell Beazley. The succinct text is by Paul Whalley, the plates by Richard Lewington. It covers over 360 species, and is small enough to slip into a shirt pocket.

Finally, as a work of reference, Volume 7 of *The Moths and Butterflies of Great Britain and Ireland* (Harley Books) is unrivalled. This volume covers all the butterflies ever recorded in Britain, including some highly unlikely species, such as Albin's Hampstead Eye. The superb plates are, once again, by Richard Lewington.

Useful addresses

Butterfly Conservation, Manor Yard, East Lulworth, Wareham, Dorset BH20 5QP. Telephone 01929 400 209; fax: 01929 400 210; e-mail: info@butterfly-conservation.org; website: www.butterfly-conservation.org

Butterfly Monitoring Scheme, Centre for Ecology and Hydrology, Monks Wood, Abbots Ripton, Huntingdon PE28 2LS. Telephone: 01487 772 400; website: www.bms.ceh.ac.uk

Watkins & Doncaster (entomological suppliers). PO Box 5, Cranbrook, Kent TN18 5EZ. Telephone 01580 753133; fax 01580 754054; e-mail robin-ford@virgin.net ; website: www.watdon.com

The Wildlife Trusts, Witham Park, Waterside South, Lincoln, Lincolnshire LN5 7JR. website: www.wildlifetrust.org.uk

The Dublin Naturalists' Field Club, 35 Nutley Park, Donnybrook, Dublin 4

Plant Health Service, Department for Environment, Food and Rural Affairs, Plant Health Division, Foss House, King's Pool, 1-2 Peasholme Green, York YO1 7PX Tel: +44 (0) 1904 45 5191/5192/5195; fax: +44 (0) 1904 45 5199 e-mail: planthealth.info@defra.gsi.gov.uk

Photographic and artwork credits

Each of the photographs used in this book is listed in this section. The following codes are used in order to save space: **ad.** = adult; **ab.** = abberant; **cat.** = chrysalis; **chr.** = chrysalis; **fem.** = female; **fpl.** = foodplant; **nect.** = nectar plant; **spr. gen.** = spring generation; **ssp.** = sub-species; **sum. gen.** = summer generation; **und.** = underside; **upp.** = upperside.

The following codes are used for photographers whose work appears frequently in the book: BG = Bob Gibbons; RR = Richard Revels; PJW = Peter J Wilson. Photographs obtained from photographic agencies are coded as follows: (NI) = (Natural Images); (WP) = (Windrush Photographs).

INTRODUCTORY SECTIONS

Frontispiece: **Red Admiral:** RR(WP).
P.6: **Small Copper:** David Carter.
P.8: **Puss Moth:** Andy Swash. **Essex Emerald moth:** Butterfly Conservation. **Dingy Skipper:** PJW. **Adonis Blue:** RR(WP). **Six-spot Burnet moth:** Andy Swash.
P.9: **Pearl-bordered Fritillary:** RR(WP). **Clouded Yellow:** RR(WP).
P.10: **High Brown Fritillary; life-cycle:** RR(WP). **Common Blue; mating pair:** Martin Warren. **Duke of Burgundy; fem.:** RR(WP). **Duke of Burgundy; hatchlings:** RR(WP). **Brimstone; pupating:** George McCarthy (WP).
P.11: **Marsh Fritillary; eggs:** RR(WP). **Glanville Fritillary; cat. web:** RR(WP).
P.12: **Marbled White; chr.:** RR(WP). **Small Tortoiseshell; bird damage:** RR(WP).
P.13: **Small Tortoiseshell; hibernating:** RR(WP).
P.14: **Black Hairstreak; chr.:** RR(WP). **Orange-tip; camouflage:** RR(WP).
P.16: **Chalkhill Blue; cat.:** RR(WP).
P.17: **Small Tortoiseshell; flying:** Andy Harmer (WP).
P.18: **Swallowtail:** PJW. **Essex Skipper:** PJW. **Grizzled Skipper:** PJW. **Wood White:** Alan Barnes. **Clouded Yellow:** RR(WP). **Brimstone:** David Carter (WP). **Large White:** Tony Hoare.
P.19: **White-letter Hairstreak:** RR (WP). **Small Copper:** RR (WP). **Silver-studded Blue:** David Carter. **Duke of Burgundy:** RR (WP). **Comma:** David Carter. **Pearl-bordered Fritillary:** RR (WP). **Meadow Brown:** RR (WP).
P.20: **Roadside verge:** BG (NI). **Rough meadow:** BG (NI).
P.21: **Downland:** BG (NI). **Woodland:** Martin Warren.
P.22: **Heathland:** BG (NI). **Upland:** BG (NI).

P.23: **Coarse grasses:** Rob Still. **Common Bird's-foot-trefoil:** BG (NI). **Common nettle:** BG (NI). **Garden:** BG (NI).
P.24: **Butterfly on camera:** Butterfly Conservation.
P.25: **Adonis Blue:** David Carter.

THE PLATES

CHEQUERED SKIPPER *Carterocephalus palaemon*
Male; upp.: RR(WP). Fem.; upp.: RR(WP). Fem.; und.: RR(WP). Egg: RR(WP). Cat.: RR(WP). Chr.: RR(WP). Fpl.; **Purple Moor-grass:** BG (NI). Nect.; **Bugle:** BG (NI).

SMALL SKIPPER *Thymelicus sylvestris*
Male; upp.: PJW. Male; und.: Martin Warren. Fem.; und.: Tony Hoare. Fem.; upp.: PJW. Egg: RR(WP). Cat.: Ken Wilmott. Chr.: Ken Wilmott. Fpl.; **Red Clover:** BG (NI).

ESSEX SKIPPER *Thymelicus lineola*
Male; upp.: RR(WP). Male; und.: PJW. Fem.; und.: Tony Hoare. Fem.; upp.: PJW. Egg: RR(WP). Cat.: RR(WP). Chr.: RR(WP): Essex & Small Skippers: males, ; showing antennae: RR(WP). Fpl.; **Red Clover:** BG (NI).

LULWORTH SKIPPER *Thymelicus acteon*
Male; upp.: PJW. Male; und.: PJW. Fem.; upp.: PJW. Fem.; und.: PJW. Egg: RR(WP). Cat.: RR(WP). Chr.: RR(WP). **Grassland, Lulworth Cove:** Rob Still.

SILVER-SPOTTED SKIPPER *Hesperia comma*
Male; upp.: PJW. Male; und.: PJW. Fem.; upp.: PJW. Fem.; und.: D Sadler. Egg: RR(WP). Cat.: RR(WP). Chr.: RR(WP). Fpl.; **Dwarf Thistle:** Peter Wilson (NI).

LARGE SKIPPER *Ochlodes venata*
Male; upp.: PJW. Male; und.: PJW. Fem.; upp.: RR(WP). Fem.; und.: PJW. Egg: RR(WP). Cat.: RR(WP). Cat.; larval tube: RR(WP). Chr.: RR(WP). Fpl.; **grasses:** Rob Still.

DINGY SKIPPER *Erynnis tages*
Male; upp.: PJW. Male; upp.; worn: PJW. Fem.; upp.: RR(WP). Fem.; upp, worn: PJW. Pair; und.; mating: RR(WP). Egg: RR(WP). Cat.: RR(WP). Chr.: RR(WP). Fpl.; **Common Bird's-foot-trefoil:** BG (NI).

GRIZZLED SKIPPER *Pyrgus malvae*
Male; upp.: PJW. Male; upp., faded: Alan Petty (WP). Fem.; upp.: RR(WP). Fem.; und.: PJW. Egg: RR(WP). Cat.: RR(WP). Chr.: RR(WP). Fpl.; **Wild Strawberry:** BG (NI).

SWALLOWTAIL *Papilio machaon*
Ad; upp.: RR(WP). Ad; und.: RR(WP). Egg: RR(WP). Cat.: RR(WP). Chr.: RR(WP). Fpl.; Milk-parsley: BG (NI).

WOOD WHITE *Leptidea sinapis*
Male; und. (sum. gen.): Frank Blackburn (WP) Ad; und. (spr. gen.): Alan Barnes. Ad; und. (spr. gen.): RR(WP). Pair; und.; mating (spr. gen.): Barry Hilling. Egg: RR(WP). Cat.: RR(WP). Chr.: RR(WP). Fpl.; Meadow Vetchling: BG (NI).

REAL'S WOOD WHITE *Leptidea reali*
Ad; und.: Robert Thompson.

CLOUDED YELLOW *Colias croceus*
Male; und.: PJW. Fem.; und., form *helice*: RR(WP). Fem.; und.: PJW. Egg: RR(WP). Cat.: RR(WP). Chr.: RR(WP). Fpl.; Red Clover: BG (NI).

BRIMSTONE *Gonepteryx rhamni*
Male; und.: PJW. Fem.; und.: PJW. Egg: RR(WP). Cat.: Martin Warren. Chr.: George McCarthy (WP). Fpl.; Alder Buckthorn: BG (NI).

LARGE WHITE *Pieris brassicae*
Male; upp. (spr. gen.): Gianpiero Ferrari. Male; upp. (sum. gen.): D Sadler. Male; und. (spr. gen.): Tony Hoare. Fem.; upp. (spr. gen.): Tony Hoare. Fem.; upp. (sum. gen.): RR(WP). Fem.; und. (sum. gen.): Tony Hoare. Egg: RR(WP). Cat.: Les Borg (WP). Chr.: Gianpiero Ferrari.

SMALL WHITE *Pieris rapae*
Male; upp. (sum. gen.): PJW. Male; und. (spr. gen.): Barry Hilling. Male; und. (sum. gen.): Martin Warren. Fem.; upp. (spr. gen.): PJW. Fem.; und. (spr. gen.): Tony Hoare. Fem.; und. (sum. gen.): Martin Warren. Egg: RR(WP). Cat.: RR(WP). Chr.: Tony Hoare.

GREEN-VEINED WHITE *Pieris napi*
Male; upp. (spr. gen.): Gianpiero Ferrari. Male; upp. (sum. gen.): RR(WP). Male; und. (spr. gen.): Barry Hilling. Male; und. (sum. gen.) Alan Barnes. Fem.; upp. (spr. gen.): BG (NI). Fem.; und. (spr. gen.): Alan Barnes. Fem.; upp. (sum. gen.): Graham Titchmarsh. Fem.; und. (sum. gen.): RR(WP). Egg: RR(WP). Cat.: RR(WP). Chr.: RR(WP). Fpl.; Water-cress: BG (NI).

ORANGE-TIP *Anthocharis cardamines*
Male; upp.: RR(WP). Male; und.: PJW. Fem.; upp.: PJW. Fem.; und.: PJW. Egg: RR(WP). Cat.: RR(WP). Chr.: Gianpiero Ferrari. Fpl.; Garlic Mustard: BG (NI).

GREEN HAIRSTREAK *Callophrys rubi*
Ad, und.: RR(WP). Ad, und.: RR(WP). Egg: Alec Harmer (NI). Cat.: RR(WP). Chr.: Gianpiero Ferrari. Fpl.; Common Bird's-foot-trefoil: BG (NI).

BROWN HAIRSTREAK *Thecla betulae*
Male; upp.: RR(WP). Male; und.: PJW. Fem.; upp.: RR(WP). Fem.; und.: RR(WP). Egg: RR(WP). Cat.: RR(WP). Chr.: RR(WP); Nect.: Fleabane: BG (NI).

PURPLE HAIRSTREAK *Quercusia quercus*
Male; upp.: RR(WP). Male; und.: RR(WP). Fem.; upp.: RR(WP). Fem.; und.: Gianpiero Ferrari. Egg: RR(WP). Cat.: RR(WP). Chr.: Gianpiero Ferrari. Fpl.; Pedunculate Oak: Rob Still.

WHITE-LETTER HAIRSTREAK *Satyrium w-album*
Male; und.: Ken Willmot. Fem.; und.: PJW. Egg: RR(WP). Cat.: RR(WP). Chr.: RR(WP). Fpl.; English Elm: BG (NI).

BLACK HAIRSTREAK *Satyrium pruni*
Male; und.: RR(WP). Fem.; und.: RR(WP). Egg: RR(WP). Cat.: RR(WP). Chr.: RR(WP). Fpl.; Blackthorn: BG (NI).

SMALL COPPER *Lycaena phlaes*
Male; upp. (top): RR(WP). Male; upp. (centre): Barry Hilling. Fem.; upp.: RR(WP). Egg: RR(WP). Cat.: RR(WP). Chr.: RR(WP).

SMALL BLUE *Cupido minimus*
Male; upp. (top): PJW. Male; upp. (centre): RR(WP). Male; und.: George McCarthy (WP). Fem.; upp.: PJW. Egg: RR(WP). Cat.: RR(WP). Chr.: Alec Harmer (NI). Fpl.; Kidney Vetch: BG (NI).

SILVER-STUDDED BLUE *Plebejus argus*
Male; upp.: PJW. Male; und. (right): RR(WP). Male; und. (bottom): David Carter. Male; und. (left), with female upp.: Frank Blackburn (WP). Fem.; upp.: D Sadler. Fem.; upp.; ssp. *caernensis*: Alec Harmer (NI). Fem.; und.: RR(WP). Egg: RR(WP). Cat.: RR(WP). Chr.: Ken Willmot

BROWN ARGUS *Aricia agestis*
Male; upp.: PJW. Male; und.: D Sadler. Fem.; upp.: RR(WP). Fem.; und.: RR(WP). Egg: RR(WP). Cat.: RR(WP). Chr.: RR(WP). Fpl.; Common Rock-rose: BG (NI).

NORTHERN BROWN ARGUS *Aricia artaxerxes*
Male; upp.; ssp. *salmacis*: D Sadler. Male; upp.; ssp. *ataxerxes*: RR(WP). Male; und.; ssp. *salmacis*: Barry Hilling. Male; und.; ssp. *ataxerxes*: Graham Titchmarsh. Fem.; upp.; ssp. *salmacis*: Alan Barnes. Fem.; upp.; ssp. *ataxerxes*: RR(WP). Fem.; und.; ssp. *salmacis*: Graham Titchmarsh. Fem.; und.; ssp. *ataxerxes*: Alec Harmer (NI). Egg: RR(WP). Cat.: RR(WP). Chr.: Alec Harmer (NI). Fpl.; Common Rock-rose: BG (NI).

COMMON BLUE *Polyommatus icarus*
Male; upp. (top): RR(WP). Male; upp. (bottom): PJW. Fem.; upp.: PJW. Fem.; upp.; ssp. *mariscolore*: RR(WP). Pair; und.; mating: Martin Warren. Ad.; und.; ab. *radiata*: RR(WP). Egg: RR(WP). Cat.: RR(WP). Chr.: RR(WP).

CHALKHILL BLUE *Lysandra coridon*
Male; upp.: RR(WP). Male; und.: RR(WP). Fem.;
upp.: PJW. Pair; und.; mating: RR(WP). Egg:
RR(WP). Cat.: RR(WP). Chr.: RR(WP). Fpl.;
Horseshoe Vetch: BG (NI).

ADONIS BLUE *Lysandra bellargus*
Male; upp.: PJW. Male; und.: PJW. Fem.; upp.:
PJW. Fem.; und.: Alan Barnes (NI). Egg: RR(WP).
Cat.: RR(WP). Chr.: Ken Willmot. Fpl.; Horseshoe
Vetch: BG (NI).

HOLLY BLUE *Celastrina argiolus*
Male; upp.: Alan Barnes. Male; und.: RR(WP).
Fem.; upp. (spr. gen.): RR(WP). Fem.; upp. (sum.
gen.): Alan Barnes. Fem.; und.: Alan Barnes. Egg:
RR(WP). Cat.: RR(WP). Chr.: RR(WP). Fpl.; Holly:
Rob Still.

LARGE BLUE *Maculinea arion*
Male; upp.: David Land. Male; und.: RR(WP).
Fem.; upp.: David Tipling (WP). Fem.; und.: Martin
Warren. Egg: Martin Warren. Cat.: Jeremy Thomas.
Chr.: Martin Warren.

DUKE OF BURGUNDY *Hamearis lucina*
Male; upp.: RR(WP). Male; und.: D Sadler. Male;
und.: Alec Harmer (NI). Fem.; upp.: RR(WP).
Fem.; und.: RR(WP). Egg: RR(WP). Cat.: RR(WP).
Chr.: RR(WP). Fpl.; Cowslip: BG (NI).

WHITE ADMIRAL *Ladoga camilla*
Male; upp.: RR(WP). Fem.; upp.: RR(WP). Ad;
und.: D Sadler. Egg: RR(WP). Cat.; 1st stage:
RR(WP). Cat.; final stage: RR(WP). Chr.: RR(WP).

PURPLE EMPEROR *Apatura iris*
Male; upp.: RR(WP). Fem.; upp.: Alan Barnes.
Pair; und.: Colin Carver. Egg: RR(WP). Cat.; 1st
stage: RR(WP). Cat.; final stage: RR(WP). Chr.:
RR(WP).

RED ADMIRAL *Vanessa atalanta*
Fem.; upp.: RR(WP). Ad.; und..: Alan Petty (WP).
Egg: Tony Hoare. Cat.: RR(WP). Chr.: RR(WP).
Fpl.; Common Nettle: Rob Still.

PAINTED LADY *Cynthia cardui.*
Male; upp.: RR(WP). Ad.; und.: Martin Warren.
Egg: RR(WP). Cat.: RR(WP). Chr.: RR(WP).

SMALL TORTOISESHELL *Aglais urticae*
Pair; upp.: RR(WP). Ad; und.: Alan Petty (WP).
Ad.; upp.; ab. *semi-ischnusoides*: RR(WP). Egg:
RR(WP). Cat.: RR(WP). Chr.: RR(WP).

PEACOCK *Inachis io*
Fem.; upp.: Butterfly Conservation. Ad; und.: PJW.
Egg: RR(WP). Cat.: RR(WP). Chr.: Gianpiero Ferrari.

COMMA *Polygonia c-album*
Male; upp.; form *hutchinsoni*: Tony Hoare. Fem.;
upp.; RR(WP). Fem.; upp.; form *hutchinsoni*:
Martin Warren. Ad; und.: RR(WP). Ad; und.: form

hutchinsoni: RR(WP). Egg: RR(WP). Cat.: RR(WP).
Chr.: Gianpiero Ferrari.

SMALL PEARL-BORDERED FRITILLARY
Boloria selene
Male; upp.: PJW. Male; und.: PJW. Fem.; upp.:
RR(WP). Fem.; upp.: RR(WP). Egg: RR(WP). Cat.:
RR(WP). Chr.: RR(WP). Fpl.; Common Dog-
violet: BG (NI).

PEARL-BORDERED FRITILLARY
Boloria euphrosyne
Male; upp.: PJW. Male; und.: PJW. Fem.; upp.:
RR(WP). Fem.; und.: RR(WP). Egg: RR(WP). Cat.:
RR(WP). Chr.: RR(WP). Fpl.; Common Dog-
violet: BG (NI).

HIGH BROWN FRITILLARY *Argynnis adippe*
Male; upp.: RR(WP). Male; und.: RR(WP). Fem.;
upp.: RR(WP). Fem.; und.: RR(WP). Egg: RR(WP).
Cat.: RR(WP). Chr.: RR(WP). Fpl.; Common Dog-
violet: BG (NI).

DARK GREEN FRITILLARY *Argynnis aglaja*
Male; upp.: RR(WP). Fem.; upp.: RR(WP). Pair;
und.; mating: Alan Petty (WP). Egg: Martin Warren.
Cat.: RR(WP). Chr.: RR(WP). Fpl.; Common Dog-
violet: BG (NI).

SILVER-WASHED FRITILLARY *Argynnis paphia*
Male; upp.: RR(WP). Male; und.: PJW. Fem.;
upp.: PJW. Fem.; upp.; form *valezina*: RR(WP) –
P.148. Male; upp.; ab. *ater*: PJW – P.148. Male;
und.; ab. *ater*: PJW – P.148. Egg: RR(WP). Cat.:
RR(WP). Chr.: RR(WP).

MARSH FRITILLARY *Eurodryas aurinia*
Male; upp.: Alan Barnes. Fem.; upp.: RR(WP).
Fem.; upp.; ssp. *hibernica*: RR(WP). Pair; und.;
mating: RR(WP). Egg: RR(WP). Cat.: RR(WP).
Chr.: RR(WP). Fpl.; Devil's-bit Scabious: BG (NI).

GLANVILLE FRITILLARY *Melitaea cinxia*
Male; upp.: Alan Barnes. Male; und.: RR(WP).
Fem.; upp.: RR(WP). Fem.; und.: RR(WP). Egg:
Tony Hoare. Cat.: RR(WP). Chr.: RR(WP). Fpl.;
Ribwort Plantain: BG (NI).

HEATH FRITILLARY *Mellicta athalia*
Pair; upp.: Alan Barnes. Pair; und.; mating: Barry
Hilling. Egg: RR(WP). Cat.: RR(WP). Chr.: RR(WP).

SPECKLED WOOD *Pararge aegeria*
Male; upp.; ssp. *oblita*: Alan Barnes. Male; und.:
Graham Titchmarsh. Fem.; upp. (spr. gen.): PJW.
Fem.; upp. (sum. gen.): BG (NI). Male; und.:
Thomas Ennis (WP). Fem.; und.: Barry Hilling. Egg:
Alec Harmer (NI). Cat.: RR(WP). Chr.: RR(WP).

WALL *Lasiommata megera*
Male; upp.: PJW. Male; und.: Graham Titchmarsh.
Fem.; upp.: PJW. Fem.; und.: Martin Warren. Egg:
RR(WP). Cat.: RR(WP). Chr.: Gianpiero Ferrari.

hutchinsoni: RR(WP). Egg: RR(WP). Cat.: RR(WP).
Chr.: Gianpiero Ferrari.

MOUNTAIN RINGLET *Erebia epiphron*
Male; upp.: RR(WP). Male; und.: PJW (NI). Fem.; upp.: RR(WP). Egg: RR(WP). Cat.: RR(WP). Chr.: RR(WP). Fpl.; Mat-grass: BG (NI).

SCOTCH ARGUS *Erebia aethiops*
Male; upp.: RR(WP). Male; und.: D Sadler. Fem.; upp.: RR(WP). Fem.; und.: RR(WP). Egg: RR(WP). Cat.: RR(WP). Chr.: RR(WP).

MARBLED WHITE *Melanargia galathea*
Male; upp.: Martin Warren. Male; und.: Barry Hilling. Fem.; upp.: RR(WP). Fem.; und.: Barry Hilling. Egg: RR(WP). Cat.: RR(WP). Chr.: RR(WP).

GRAYLING *Hipparchia semele*
Male; und.: PJW. Fem.; upp.: PJW. Fem.; und., on Heather: RR(WP). Fem.; und., on ground: PJW. Egg: Ken Willmot. Cat.: RR(WP). Chr.: RR(WP). Fpl.; Sheep's-fescue: BG (NI).

GATEKEEPER *Pyronia tithonus*
Male; upp.: PJW. Fem.; upp.: PJW. Pair; und.; mating: Barry Hilling. Egg: RR(WP). Cat.: Gianpiero Ferrari. Chr.: RR(WP). Fpl.; grasses: Rob Still.

MEADOW BROWN *Maniola jurtina*
Male; upp.: RR(WP). Male; und.: RR(WP). Fem.; upp.: PJW. Pair; und., mating: Alan Barnes. Egg: Ken Willmot. Cat.: RR(WP). Chr.: RR(WP). Fpl.; grasses: Rob Still.

RINGLET *Aphantopus hyperantus*
Male; upp.: PJW. Male; und.: PJW. Fem.; upp.: RR(WP). Fem.; und.: PJW. Ad; und.; ab. *arete*: RR(WP). Ad; und.; ab. *lanceolata*: RR(WP). Egg: Ken Willmot. Cat.: RR(WP). Chr.: RR(WP). Fpl.; grasses: Rob Still.

SMALL HEATH *Coenonympha pamphilus*
Fem.; und.: PJW. Fem.; und.: RR(WP). Pair; und.; mating: Trevor Codlin. Egg: RR(WP). Cat.: RR(WP). Chr.: RR(WP). Fpl.; grasses: Rob Still.

LARGE HEATH *Coenonympha tullia*
Ad; und.; ssp. *scotica*: Alan Barnes. Male; und.; ssp. *polydama*: Gianpiero Ferrari. Fem.; und.; ssp. *polydama*: D Sadler. Fem.; und.; ssp. *polydama*: PJW. Male; und.; ssp. *davus*: Alan Barnes. Fem.; und.; ssp. *davus*: RR(WP). Egg: RR(WP). Cat.: RR(WP). Chr.: RR(WP).

LARGE COPPER *Lycaena dispar*
Male; upp.: RR(WP). Fem.; upp.: RR(WP). Fem.; und.: RR(WP). Pair; und.; mating: RR(WP). Egg: RR(WP). Cat.: RR(WP). Chr.: RR(WP).

BLACK-VEINED WHITE *Aporia crataegi*
Male; upp.: RR(WP). Male; und.: RR(WP). Cat.: RR(WP). Chr.: RR(WP).

LARGE TORTOISESHELL *Nymphalis polychloros*
Ad; upp.: Alan Barnes. Fem.; und.: Gianpiero Ferrari. Cat.: Alan Barnes. Chr.: Gianpiero Ferrari.

QUEEN OF SPAIN FRITILLARY
Argynnis lathonia
Fem.; upp.: RR(WP). Ad; und.: RR(WP). Cat.: Gianpiero Ferrari. Chr.: Gianpiero Ferrari.

BERGER'S CLOUDED YELLOW
Colias alfacarensis
Male; und.: RR(WP). Cat.: RR(WP).

PALE CLOUDED YELLOW *Colias hyale*
Fem.; und.: RR(WP). Cat.: RR(WP).

BATH WHITE *Pontia daplidice*
Fem.; upp.: RR(WP). Fem.; und.: RR(WP). Cat.: RR(WP).

CAMBERWELL BEAUTY *Nymphalis antiopa*
Fem.; upp.: RR(WP).

SHORT-TAILED BLUE *Everes argiades*
Male; upp.: RR(WP). Fem.; upp.: Martin Warren. Fem.; und.: RR(WP).

LONG-TAILED BLUE *Lampides boeticus*
Fem.; upp.: RR(WP). Fem.; und.: RR(WP).

MAZARINE BLUE *Polyommatus semiargus*
Male; upp.: Martin Warren. Fem.; upp.: Martin Warren. Male; und.: Martin Warren.

MONARCH *Danaus plexippus*
Fem.; upp.: RR(WP). Ad; und.: RR(WP).

The photographs of the eggs, caterpillars and chrysali on pages 169-178 are included with the relevant species above.

Plants and animals mentioned in the text

PLANT SPECIES

Agrimony *Agrimonia eupatoria*
Alder Buckthorn *Frangula alnus*
Ash *Fraxinus excelsior*
Aubretia *Aubrieta* sp.

Bell Heather *Erica cinerea*
bents *Agrostis* spp.
Betony *Betonica officinalis*
Bilberry *Vaccinium myrtillus*
birches *Betula* spp.
Black Medick *Medicago lupulina*
Blackthorn *Prunus spinosa*
Blue Moor-grass *Sesleria caerulea*
Bluebell *Hyacinthoides non-scripta*
Bracken *Pteridium aquilinum*
Bramble *Rubus fruticosus* agg.
brassicas *Brassicaceae*
Bristle Bent *Agrostis curtisii*
Broom *Cytisus scoparius*
Brussels-sprouts *Brassica oleracea*
Buckthorn *Rhamnus catharticus*
buddleias *Buddleja* spp.
Bugle *Ajuga reptans*
buttercups *Ranunculus* spp.

Cabbage *Brassica oleracea*
Charlock *Sinapis arvensis*
clovers *Trifolium* spp.
Cock's-foot *Dactylis glomerata*
Common Bird's-foot-trefoil *Lotus corniculatus*
Common Couch *Elytrigia repens*
Common Cow-wheat *Melampyrum pratense*
Common Dog-violet *Viola riviniana*
Common Nettle *Urtica dioica*
Common Restharrow *Ononis repens*
Common Rock-rose *Helianthemum nummularium*
Common Sorrel *Rumex acetosa*
Common Stork's-bill *Erodium cicutarium*
cottongrasses *Eriophorum* spp.
Cowslip *Primula veris*

crane's-bills *Geranium* spp.
Creeping Cinquefoil *Potentilla reptans*
Creeping Soft-grass *Holcus mollis*
Creeping Thistle *Cirsium arvense*
Cross-leaved Heath *Erica tetralix*
Cuckooflower *Cardamine pratensis*
currants *Ribes* spp.

dandelions *Taraxacum* spp.
Devil's-bit Scabious *Succisa pratensis*
Dog-rose *Rosa canina*
Dogwood *Cornus sanguinea*
Dove's-foot Crane's-bill *Geranium molle*
Dwarf Thistle *Cirsium acaule*

Early Hair-grass *Aira praexox*
elms *Ulmus* spp.
English Elm *Ulmus procera*
eyebrights *Euphrasia* spp.

False Brome *Brachypodium sylvaticum*
fescues *Festuca* spp.
Field Maple *Acer campestre*
Field Pansy *Viola arvensis*
(Common) Fleabane *Pulicaria dysenterica*
forget-me-nots *Myosotis* spp.
Foxglove *Digitalis purpurea*
French Marigold *Tagetes patula*

Garlic Mustard *Alliaria petiolata*
geraniums *Pelargonium* spp.
Germander Speedwell *Veronica chaemaedrys*
Goat Willow *Salix caprea*
Gorse *Ulex europaeus*
Greater Bird's-foot-trefoil *Lotus pedunculatus*
Grey Willow *Salix cinerea*

Hairy Violet *Viola hirta*
Hare's-tail Cottongrass *Eriophorum vaginatum*
hawkbits *Leontodon* spp.
hawthorns *Crataegus* spp.
Hazel *Corylus avellana*

Heather *Calluna vulgaris*
Hedge Mustard *Sisymbrium officinale*
Hemp-agrimony *Eupatorium canabinum*
Holly *Ilex aquifolium*
Honesty *Lunaria annua*
Honeysuckle *Lonicera periclymenum*
Hop *Humulus lupulus*
Horseshoe Vetch *Hippocrepis comosa*

Ivy *Hedera helix*

Kale *Brassica oleracea*
Kidney Vetch *Anthyllis vulneraria*
knapweeds *Centaurea* spp. and *Acroptilon* spp.

Lavender *Lavandula* x *intermedia*
Lobelia *Lobelia erinus*
Lucerne *Medicago sativa*

Mange-tout pea *Pisum sativum*
marjoram *Origanum* sp.
Marram *Ammophila arenaria*
Marsh Thistle *Cirsium palustre*
Marsh Violet *Viola palustris*
Mat-grass *Nardus stricta*
Meadow Vetchling *Lathyrus pratensis*
meadow-grasses *Poa* spp.
Milk-parsley *Peucedanum palustre*
milkweed *Asclepias* spp.

Nasturtium *Tropaeolum majus*
nettles *Urtica* spp.

oaks *Quercus* spp.
Oil-seed Rape *Brassica napus*

Pedunculate Oak *Quercus robur*
Primrose *Primula vulgaris*
Purple Moor-grass *Molinia caerulea*

Ragged-Robin *Lychnis flos-cuculi*
ragworts *Senecio* spp.
Red Clover *Trifolium pratense*
Red Fescue *Festuca rubra*
Ribwort Plantain *Plantago lanceolata*
scabious *Knautia* spp. and *Scabiosa* spp.

Sheep's Sorrel *Rumex acetosella*
Sheep's-fescue *Festuca ovina*
Silverweed *Potentilla anserina*
Small-leaved Elm *Ulmus minor*
Sweet-William *Dianthus barbatus*

teasels *Dipsacus* spp.
thistles *Cirsium* spp. and *Carduus* spp.
Thrift *Armeria maritima*
Timothy *Phleum pratense*
Tor-grass *Brachypodium pinnatum*
Tormentil *Potentilla erecta*
Tufted Vetch *Vicia cracca*

Valerian *Valeriana* spp. or *Centranthus* spp.
violets *Viola* spp.

Water Dock *Rumex hydrolapathum*
Water-cress *Rorippa nasturtium-aquaticum*
Wavy Hair-grass *Deschampsia flexuosa*
Wild Marjoram *Origanum vulgare*
Wild Mignonette *Reseda lutea*
Wild Pansy *Viola tricolor*
Wild Privet *Ligustrum vulgare*
Wild Strawberry *Fragaria vesca*
Wild Thyme *Thymus polytrichus*
willows *Salix* spp.
Wych Elm *Ulmus glabra*

Yorkshire-fog *Holcus lanatus*

INVERTEBRATE SPECIES
ant (black) *Lasius alienus*
ant (black) *Lasius niger*
ant (red) *Myrmica sabuleti*
Burnet Companion (moth) *Euclidia glyphica*
ichneumon wasp *Listrodomus nycthemerus*
Mother Shipton (moth) *Callistege mi*

VERTEBRATE SPECIES
Muntjac (deer) *Muntiacus muntjak*
Rabbit *Oryctolagus cuniculus*
Spotted Flycatcher *Muscicapa striata*
Great Tit *Parus major*

Acknowledgements

Many people have contributed to the production of this book and our sincere thanks are due to them all. It is our intention that everyone who has contributed to the book is named in this section, but if we have inadvertently missed anyone we can only apologise. Despite the contributions of others, we hold full responsibility for any errors that may have crept in, and for any omissions which we may have made.

The production of this book would not have been possible without the help and co-operation of the photographers whose work is featured here. The plates are one of the key features of the book and we would like to acknowledge the skill and patience of the following photographers who kindly allowed us to use their work: Alan Barnes; Frank Blackburn; Les Borg; David Carter; Colin Carver; Trevor Codlin; Thomas Ennis; Gianpiero Ferrari; Bob Gibbons; Andy Harmer; Alec Harmer; Barry Hilling; Tony Hoare; David Land; George McCarthy; Alan Petty; Richard Revels; Dave Sadler; Rob Still; Andy Swash; Jeremy Thomas; Robert Thompson; David Tipling; Graham Titchmarsh; Martin Warren; Ken Wilmott; and Peter J. Wilson. who took the great majority of the photographs. The name of the photographer who took each photograph is shown in the photographic credits section of this book which starts on page 184 We would particularly like to thank Richard Revels and Peter J Wilson who took a large number of the photographs. Thanks are also due to David Tipling of Windrush Photographs, who went to considerable trouble in finding suitable photographs of some of the more elusive species, to Bob Gibbons of Natural Image for supplying photographs of the foodplants and to Butterfly Conservation for allowing us to use some of the photographs from their collection. We must also thank all those photographers who took the time and trouble to send their photographs for possible inclusion. We received many photographs of a very high standard and the choice of photographs made has been down to the requirements of the plate. It is fair to say that there were many more photographs we would have liked to have used if space permitted. Lastly thanks to David and Terry at Max Communications for their help with the scanning of the images

We are grateful to Butterfly Conservation, for allowing us to draw heavily on the information included in The Millennium Atlas of Butterflies in Britain and Ireland.

We would like to particularly thank Richard Fox and Martin Warren of Butterfly Conservation for undertaking a technical edit of the book in its latter stages of production and Andy Swash for collating most of the photographs and undertaking a final edit of the text.

We would also like to thank David Bridges and Julie McGloin of Butterfly Conservation for their patience and enthusiasm for the project.

Rob Still would also like to thank his wife Penny, and his daughters Rachel and Anya for their support throughout the project and their understanding when faced with many a 'dad's doing the book' weekend.

Index of English and scientific names

Figures in **bold text** refer to the page number on which the main text and facing page plate for the species can be found. Figures in plain text relate to other pages where the species is mentioned, Italicised text indicate pages numbers where there the species is depicted.